YORK NOTE

# THE PICTURE OF DORIAN GRAY

## OSCAR WILDE

## NOTES BY FRANCES GRAY

 Longman

 York Press

The right of Frances Gray to be identified as Author of
this Work has been asserted by her in accordance
with the Copyright, Designs and Patents Act 1988

YORK PRESS
322 Old Brompton Road, London SW5 9JH

PEARSON EDUCATION LIMITED
Edinburgh Gate, Harlow,
Essex CM20 2JE, United Kingdom
Associated companies, branches and representatives throughout the world

© Librairie du Liban *Publishers* 2009

Quotations from *The Picture of Dorian Gray* by Oscar Wilde are from the
Wordsworth Classics edition (1992, 2001)

10 9 8 7 6

ISBN 978–1–4082–1731–3

Phototypeset by Carnegie Publishing

Printed in China (EPC/06)

# CONTENTS

## Part Five
### Background

## INTRODUCTION

## STUDYING NOVELS

Reading novels and exploring them critically can be approached in a number of ways, but when reading the text for the first time it is a good idea to consider some, or all, of the following:

- **Format and style**: how do novels differ from other genres? How are chapters or other divisions used to reveal information? Is there a **narrator**, and if so, how does he or she convey both his or her emotions and those of the characters?

- **The writer's perspective**: consider what the writer has to say, how he or she presents a particular view of people, the world, society, ideas, issues, etc. Are, or were, these views controversial?

- **Shape and structure**: explore how the **narrative** of the story develops – the moments of revelation and reflection, openings and endings, conflicts and resolutions. Is there one main plot or are there multiple plots and sub-plots?

- **Setting**: where and when is the novel set? How do the locations shape or reflect the lives and relationships of the characters? What does the setting add in terms of tone?

- **Choice of language**: does the writer choose to write formally or informally? Does he or she use different registers for characters and narrators, and employ language features such as **imagery** and dialect?

- **Links and connections**: what other texts does this novel remind you of? Can you see connections between its narrative, characters and ideas and those of other texts you have studied? Is the novel part of a tradition or literary movement?

- **Your perspective and that of others**: what are your feelings about the novel? Can you relate to the narrators, characters, themes and ideas? What do others say about it – for example, critics, or other writers?

These York Notes offer an introduction to *The Picture of Dorian Gray* and cannot substitute for close reading of the text and the study of secondary sources.

**CHECK THE BOOK**

Peter Ackroyd's novel *The Last Testament of Oscar Wilde* (1984) imagines Wilde's last months. His careful use of Wilde's vocabulary and sentence structure shows how a novel can also offer new critical insights.

**CHECK THE NET**

The Victorian Web at **www.victorianweb.org** is an excellent resource for nineteenth-century material on history, philosophy, politics and the arts.

# READING *THE PICTURE OF DORIAN GRAY*

In the dying years of the nineteenth century, a handful of novels appeared whose characters are familiar all over the western world: Dracula, the vampire; Dr Jekyll and his evil second self, Mr Hyde; Sherlock Holmes the detective; and Dorian Gray, the beautiful young man whose picture grows old and ugly in his place. They are known not only through their original texts but in freely adapted versions from operas to graphic novels. They acquired their extraordinary power by articulating the deepest anxieties of the late Victorians and they continue to offer us ways to interpret our own experience.

Of all these texts, *The Picture of Dorian Gray* had the most complex relationship with its early public. It attracted passionate and widely polarised responses. Wilde's wife complained that 'since Oscar wrote [it] no one will speak to us' (Linda Dryden, *The Modern Gothic and Literary Doubles*, 2003, p. 117). It became evidence in the criminal courts: during Wilde's attempt to sue the Marquess of Queensberry for libel and his subsequent appearance in the dock as one of the first people to be tried for consenting homosexual activity, the prosecution described it as an 'immoral and indecent work' (Hyde, p. 114) and the defence as 'an allegory pure and simple' (Hyde, p. 230). Wilde was frequently identified with his murderous, beautiful and fabulously wealthy central character, despite being none of these things. Meanwhile, Dorian Gray himself was awarded the title 'Man of the Day' by *Vanity Fair* magazine, which carried a full-length picture of him modelling a stylish dressing gown, his fictional status apparently no bar to this honour.

While over the next century society came to regret its persecution of Wilde, and to undo some of the legislation that led to it, his book has tended to be undervalued. Because the central character has a number of relationships which are – to modern readers – obviously homosexual, it has been treated as little more than a carefully constructed code to discuss what its contemporaries considered unsayable, and a tale that may have outgrown its usefulness in a less censored world. Because the story was unashamedly aimed at a popular readership – first appearing in the kind of magazine one of the new commuter class might read on the train – it has been

## CHECK THE BOOK

*The Trials of Oscar Wilde* (edited by H. Montgomery Hyde) was first published by William Hodge and Co., in the Notable British Trials series, in 1948.

## CONTEXT

New and cheaper printing technologies evolving from the 1860s to the 1890s led to the appearance of a rush of periodicals. Probably the most famous was the *Strand Magazine,* a monthly fiction magazine founded by George Newnes. It was first published in the UK in January 1891 and was immediately popular, with an initial sale of nearly 300,000.

dismissed as sensationalist horror. Because it is packed with **allusions** to other literature from the King James Bible to French novels, it has been written off as derivative. Wilde himself, with his apparently airy assertion in the preface that 'All art is quite useless' (p. 4), has not helped its reputation. But, as the novelist Joyce Carol Oates remarks, readers are 'always saying about *Dorian Gray*, with an air of surprise, that the novel is exceptionally good after all' (quoted in Norton Edition, p. 423).

It is exceptional because it cannot be pinned down. Steeped in classical mythology at Oxford and in Celtic folklore during his Dublin childhood, Wilde grounded his **narrative** in some of the oldest stories of all: tales about appearance and reality, like *Beauty and the Beast*; myths about doomed seekers for eternal life, like Tithonus; stories of people snatched away to the Irish fairy kingdom, Tir Nan Og, emerging after what felt like days to find that years had passed and everyone they knew had aged or died. Two stories above all echo and re-echo through the book and inform its structure and **imagery**. The first is the legend of Faust, who sold his soul to the devil in exchange for knowledge, and after twenty-four years was dragged down to Hell, unable to repent. The second is the story of Narcissus, the beautiful young man who was doomed from the moment he saw his own reflection in a pool and pined away in hopeless desire.

Like all myths, *Dorian Gray* has a simple structure, but the issues it raises are complex. Wilde explained to a hostile reviewer in the *Scots Observer* that he wanted to keep the atmosphere 'vague and indeterminate and wonderful' (*Selected Letters of Oscar Wilde*, ed. Rupert Hart-Davis, 1979, p. 82) to prevent too simple a moral being drawn. His fantastic tale is set within a sharply observed Victorian world, moving from country houses where aristocrats amuse themselves at shooting parties to East End slums haunted by prostitutes and opium addicts. At times Wilde's book is as unsparingly realistic as any explicitly political novel of the period; at others it employs a stylised **comedy** in which impossibly sophisticated lovers exchange the witty banter that made Wilde the most successful playwright of his day after he decided that his *Dorian Gray* royalties were inadequate and turned to the theatre.

**CONTEXT**

Tithonus was one of the most tragic figures of classical myth. When Aurora, the Dawn, became his lover, she asked the gods to give him eternal life. However, she forgot to ask for eternal youth to accompany it.

**CHECK THE BOOK**

Christopher Marlowe's play *Doctor Faustus* (c. 1590) shows Faustus selling his soul for twenty-four years of knowledge and pleasure, arranged by the devil Mephistopheles. He is constantly urged to repent by a Good Angel and told by a Bad Angel that there is no way back. At the end Faustus is torn in pieces by devils. *Dorian Gray* draws closely on the structure of the play (see **Structure and narrative**).

**CHECK THE POEM**

The story of Narcissus was told by the poet Ovid in his work *Metamorphoses* around AD 4. An excellent translation can be found in Ted Hughes's *Tales from Ovid* (1997).

**CONTEXT**

New technologies had shown how to record people's voices on wax cylinders and their appearance on photographic plates – Wilde was captured on both – and these seemed almost magical in their power, allowing ordinary people to 'own' a piece of the subject, whether a famous criminal or Queen Victoria.

**CONTEXT**

In the early days of police photography, it was customary to photograph the eyes of murder victims as it was believed that they would retain an image of the killer.

We often hear that we live in an age obsessed with image. Magazines show glamorous photographs of celebrities but also feature snapshots of their awkward moments, as if to imply that this is what they are 'really' like. As *Dorian Gray* reveals, this double-sided preoccupation with image is not new. The Victorians were fascinated by the relationship between face and mask. They demanded high standards of decorum – but the age was rocked by sexual scandals and the hypocrisy that preached hard work while paying starvation wages. Dorian himself, covering up debauchery behind an innocent face, could serve as a symbol for his time.

The major characters have a curious relationship with Dorian's image even before he makes his fatal wish. Basil, the artist, is cautious about showing it – partly because he thinks it reveals something about himself and his passion for the subject. But he also describes it as 'the real Dorian' (p. 26) and seems to feel that keeping the name of the sitter to himself is to possess control over who and what Dorian is. Lord Henry tries to buy the picture: when this attempt fails, he acquires a large number of photographs of Dorian – and we do not know whether his motive is power or desire.

Dorian is able to betray so many people because they find him, as Basil does, someone whose 'personality was so fascinating that, if I allowed it to do so, it would absorb my whole nature, my whole soul, my very art itself' (p. 9). 'Personality' – a word made popular by Wilde – is the self as it is manifest in the world, in the way a person chooses to interact with his or her social group. A good performance of one's personality can oil the wheels of society and make life more fun – but it can also be a way of masking selfishness and cruelty, as the more vulnerable characters in Wilde's witty **social comedies** come to understand. In *Dorian Gray* we see Lord Henry and Dorian acting out social roles in their claustrophobic world. Dorian finds other outlets through which to express himself, but rather than enlarging his experience in order to challenge the hypocrisy of his own world, he uses his social self as a cover, putting on a dinner jacket and a witty front after committing murder.

Dorian evades the law, the censure of his peers and the results of sexual irresponsibility. Implicitly, this challenges us to consider an important question about the basis of morality: will we only do the right thing in order to avoid punishment, or do we have a conscience that urges us towards goodness? The cynical Lord Henry declares, 'Conscience and cowardice are really the same things' (p. 9). The charitable Basil disagrees. At times, Dorian seems to confirm Lord Henry's view, afraid of 'what the neighbours will say', like any Victorian hypocrite skulking behind lace curtains. But while it is not surprising that he fears social ostracism, prison or the death penalty – all of which he risks in the course of the story – his terror seems to go beyond rational fear. It seems to lie in the actual *visibility* of the picture. He has the idea that, whatever social roles he chooses to play, the sum total of every vicious thing he has done is concentrated on a single square of canvas. Dorian's crimes are not likely to be found out or punished, but the image of what he has become has the capacity to terrify him just by being there.

Wilde does not force upon us any particular point of view about the self, the soul or morality, and this is what makes the book so endlessly readable. It is packed with ideas about the relationships between self and other, body and soul, image and reality, but it leaves us to draw our own conclusions. The **narrative** is full of pithy remarks about all these issues – which are often contradicted by the events of the plot only a few pages later. Characters who act wickedly expound political or social views disconcertingly full of humane wisdom. The chief character commits terrible sins – but Wilde refuses to tell us what they are. As he wrote to one of his critics, 'Each man sees his own sin in Dorian Gray. What Dorian Gray's sins are no one knows. He who finds them has brought them' (Hart-Davis, p. 82).

It is also a book full of beguiling sensual images, with a wonderful zest for art, food, fabrics, music and jokes. In the last years of his life, poor and in exile, Wilde was still preoccupied with the fine detail of his own texts – the words and the quality of the paper – and with pleasure. He signs off a letter about the proofs of his last major work, *The Ballad of Reading Gaol*, with a cocky little flourish: '*Dorian Gray* is a classic, and deservedly. Excuse this brief letter. I am in a hurry to buy cigarettes' (Hart-Davis, p. 318).

 **QUESTION**

Wilde famously stated that 'Basil Hallward is what I think I am: Lord Henry, what the world thinks me: Dorian, what I would like to be – in other ages, perhaps' (Hart-Davis, p. 116). To what extent can the three central characters be seen as mirrors of one another?

**CONTEXT**

Shortly after leaving prison Wilde expressed nostalgia for the 'old days of power and personality' (Hart-Davis, p. 316). He was referring to his habit of demanding proof copies of his work on the paper that would be used in the published edition, suggesting that 'personality' was for him closely bound up with the expression of one's art.

## PART TWO

## THE TEXT

### NOTE ON THE TEXT

The edition used in these Notes is the 2001 Wordsworth Classics Edition edited by John M. L. Drew. The text is taken from the first illustrated version published in Paris in 1908, which was essentially the same as Wilde's 1891 version of *The Picture of Dorian Gray* published by Ward, Lock and Company. It differs in many respects from the original story for *Lippincott's Magazine*, published in 1890, and you may find it useful to consult an edition offering both versions, such as Donald L. Lawler's Norton Edition (1988), which also comments on Wilde's revisions to his original typescript.

### SYNOPSIS

The novel begins with a Preface, which in a series of provocative statements invites the reader to think about the relationship between art and life. As the story begins, artist Basil Hallward is putting the finishing touches to a portrait of a beautiful young man, watched by his friend Lord Henry Wotton. Lord Henry gradually draws from Basil the admission that he is obsessed by the subject, Dorian Gray. Dorian arrives for a sitting and is mesmerised by Lord Henry, who urges him to defy social strictures and make the most of his youth by exploring every thought and sensation. Faced with the completed picture, Dorian is aware for the first time of his own beauty and appalled at the thought of losing it. He says he would give his soul if the picture could age while he remained young.

Dorian begins to forsake Basil's company for Lord Henry's. Soon he is in love with a wonderfully talented young actress, Sibyl Vane. They become engaged, and Dorian invites both Basil and Lord Henry to the shabby theatre where she is playing Juliet. Sibyl knows Dorian only as 'Prince Charming'. Her brother James, who is shortly leaving England, warns her to be on her guard.

Sibyl's performance as Juliet is terrible. When Dorian goes backstage, Sibyl tells him that now she understands the reality of love she can no longer pretend emotions she does not feel, and urges him to take her away from the theatre. Coldly, he tells her he never wants to see her again. Returning home, Dorian finds that his portrait wears an expression of cruelty. He is horrified, and decides that he will go back to Sibyl and marry her. The next morning he writes a long letter asking her forgiveness. Lord Henry visits Dorian to break the news that Sibyl has killed herself – and persuades Dorian to go with him to the opera.

Basil is shocked at Dorian's new callousness. He tells Dorian that he intends to exhibit the portrait. Dorian draws a confession of love from Basil, but refuses to allow the picture to be seen by anyone, even Basil, and hides it in his old attic schoolroom.

Wanting distraction, Dorian asks Lord Henry for something to read, and receives a book that is to colour his whole life. He begins to imitate its hero, exploring a world of sensations and imagining himself into the minds of some of the great sinners of history. Eighteen years pass, and he acquires a sinister reputation, but his innocent young face leads people to discount the rumours. Basil, about to leave for Paris, pays a late-night visit to find out the truth.

Dorian takes Basil to the attic to see 'his soul' – the portrait, now hideously corrupt. As Basil urges him to repent, Dorian stabs him, and the next day summons a former friend, Alan Campbell, and blackmails him into disposing of the body. The evidence gone, Dorian continues his double life, flirting at society parties and visiting opium dens in the East End. There, Sibyl's brother James, who has been stalking him, hears Dorian addressed as 'Prince Charming' and tracks him to his country house, Selby Royal. Here James is accidentally killed during a shooting party.

Dorian is now safe, but finds himself increasingly afraid. He tells Lord Henry that he intends to change, and has performed a 'virtuous' act in deciding not to seduce a young country girl who resembles Sibyl. Lord Henry is sceptical. Dorian goes home to see if his portrait bears any sign of change: its face now wears the leer of a hypocrite. Wildly, Dorian stabs it with the knife that killed Basil.

**CONTEXT**

Ironically, Dorian's looks closely resemble those of Wilde's destructive lover Lord Alfred Douglas (see **Oscar Wilde's life and works**). The first remark 'Bosie' Douglas addressed to Wilde was a request for him to autograph his copy of the book.

A cry is heard. The servants break into the room and discover a portrait of the beautiful young Dorian. On the floor is the body of a hideous old man with a knife in his heart.

## DETAILED SUMMARIES

### PREFACE

- Wilde presents a list of epigrams on the function of the critic, the nature of art and the role of the artist in the nineteenth century.
- Wilde signs the Preface with his own name.

The list of **epigrams** opens with the definition of the artist as 'the creator of beautiful things' (p. 3) and goes on to suggest that the critic does not so much evaluate art as reveal himself through his opinions. It then accuses the age of an inability to appreciate either **realism** or **romanticism**. It explores the technical and emotional tools of the artist, which rather than having an inherent moral quality are related to fitness of purpose. It avers that the critic must, although it is risky, look at both what is on the surface and the deeper symbolic function of the work of art. It does not expect a unified response to any work of art – disagreement is healthy – and maintains that art has no use. Wilde adds his own name to the end.

### COMMENTARY

This Preface was Wilde's first substantial addition to the story as it appeared in *Lippincott's Magazine*. It was partly inserted to anticipate and rebut some of the accusations of 'immorality' that *Dorian Gray* had already attracted in its earlier form. However, it does more than this. Victorian writings on art tended to consist of ponderous volumes like Ruskin's *Modern Painters*. This series of short and snappy epigrams looks almost cheeky in comparison. Placed at the beginning of the **narrative**, like a manifesto, it seems to constitute a challenge to the reader. Before we are allowed to plunge into the narrative, we are expected to think, and to abandon some preconceptions.

**CHECK THE BOOK**

An American contemporary of Wilde's, Mark Twain, shared his sense of personal style and epigrammatic wit, although Twain adopted a folksy exterior rather than Wilde's dandyism. Twain's 1894 novel *Pudden'head Wilson*, in which a man considered foolish because of his fondness for pithy and paradoxical sayings uncovers a mystery, prefaces each chapter with an epigram from 'Pudden'head Wilson's Calendar'.

The fifth epigram reads: 'The nineteenth-century dislike of Realism is the rage of Caliban seeing his own face in a glass. The nineteenth-century dislike of Romanticism is the rage of Caliban not seeing his own face in a glass' (p. 3). That is, when confronted with a lifelike account of the world such as that produced by Realist novelists, readers reacted in horror and refused to recognise the truth of what they read. But when challenged by a work of art in a more fantastic vein, they dismissed it as irrelevant to them (see **Literary background: Realism versus Romance**). The careful balance of these sentences suggests that we are going to meet both narrative styles and will have to find some way of reconciling them. Given that 'the highest, as the lowest, form of criticism is a mode of autobiography' (p. 3), we can expect our response to the book to teach us something about ourselves.

Sometimes the Preface seems to be stating the obvious – 'The artist is the creator of beautiful things' – as if Wilde thinks that we cannot take contemporary views for granted, but must go back to the basics. Sometimes it is provocative – 'There is no such thing as a moral or an immoral book' (p. 3). Sometimes it is flippant – 'All art is quite useless' (p. 4). But the text warns us that things are not always what they appear on the surface. Some of these lines will reappear in the mouths of particular characters, and will seem to mean something quite different.

Perhaps the most useful way to treat the Preface is to turn back to it periodically as you read. Ask yourself whether your understanding of a word like 'beautiful' or 'useless' is changing, or consider how a Victorian reader might modify his or her definitions, or how the major characters might respond at different stages in the narrative. It will become apparent that, as Wilde says, to go beneath the surface is risky, but none the less rewarding for that.

**CHECK THE BOOK**

There is an excellent and detailed analysis of the Preface to *Dorian Gray* in Bruce Michelson's *Literary Wit* (2000).

**CONTEXT**

After some censorious reviews of the *Lippincott's* version of *Dorian Gray*, Wilde wrote to one editor: 'That the editor of the *St James's Gazette* should employ Caliban as his art-critic was possibly natural' (Hart-Davis, p. 82).

**QUESTION**

Choose any of the statements in the *Preface*. What light does it throw on the story of Dorian?

---

**GLOSSARY**

| | |
|---|---|
| 3 | **elect** the chosen, a word often used with religious overtones – perhaps 'chosen' here rather than 'elite' to imply that such ability has nothing to do with class |
| | **Caliban** a character from Shakespeare's *The Tempest*, the resentful offspring of a witch, who is kept by the magician Prospero as an uneducated slave |

## CHAPTER 1

- Lord Henry, visiting Basil Hallward's studio, sees the artist's painting of Dorian Gray.
- Basil refuses to sell a work that contains so much of himself.
- He is reluctant to let Lord Henry meet Dorian, but Dorian arrives at the studio.

Lord Henry Wotton is visiting his artist friend Basil Hallward, who is completing a portrait of a beautiful young man. Lord Henry urges Basil to exhibit it, but the artist replies that it contains 'too much of myself' (p. 6). He does not intend to divulge the name of the subject, and tells Lord Henry that anything that makes a person stand out from the crowd – Lord Henry's wealth, his own talent or the beauty of the sitter, Dorian Gray – is a danger.

Pressed, Basil recounts his first meeting with Dorian at the house of a mutual acquaintance. He now sees Dorian's presence as vital to his artistic power, the source of his vision of 'an entirely new mode of style' (p. 12). Lord Henry presses him for an introduction. Basil points out that Lord Henry might not see Dorian in the same way, and reiterates his unwillingness to exhibit a picture so clearly revealing his 'idolatry' (p. 12). Lord Henry is sceptical about this sentiment and recalls that he and Dorian share a social circle, though they have not met. Basil wishes that this should remain so, but the butler now announces Dorian. Basil asks Lord Henry not to influence his friend's 'simple and ... beautiful nature' (p. 15), and receives the non-committal reply 'What nonsense you talk!' (p. 15).

## COMMENTARY

The opening of the novel is sensuously descriptive and seems to set a leisurely pace. However, a key theme is already being established – the interplay between art and nature. There is a constant shifting of sensations between the studio, the place of art, and the garden, the place of nature. The bird-shadows on the silk curtains may be real, creating the illusion that they are painted, or painted, creating the illusion that they are real, and the sound of the city is transformed

**CHECK THE BOOK**

Theophile Gautier's novel *Mademoiselle de Maupin* (1835–6) has a famous preface in which the author attacks the vogue for moralistic literature and maintains that the point of art is to enhance the joy of life.

into organ music. This theme is further developed by the description of the setting Basil has devised for himself. Wilde based it on the studio of his friend Charles Ricketts, who designed the original cover for *Dorian Gray*. The 'divan of Persian saddlebags' (p. 5) reflects the East of the Victorian **orientalist** imagination, a place of drugs and erotic pleasures. Basil's art will evidently have some kind of relationship with the idea of pleasure – possibly forbidden pleasure.

There is, too, a flicker of something sinister in the **allusion** to Basil's 'sudden disappearance some years ago' (p. 5). So brief that it is easily overlooked, this casual planting of a clue is typical of a genre new to the nineteenth century, the detective story. It implies that conflict may not be confined to a conversation but may be violently acted out. There is a hint that this may be a tragic novel, with Basil's remark 'there is a fatality about all physical and intellectual distinction' (p. 6). Tragedy is often associated with over-reaching ambition, and Basil is at the peak of his career. His success is not only commercial – although the luxuries in his studio suggest that he does have success of this kind – but also intellectual.

Basil's project, inspired by his relationship with Dorian, is ambitious: to create a synthesis of two schools (see **Literary background: The English Aesthetics**). But Dorian is also associated with arrogance and its fall by Lord Henry's praise of him as an 'Adonis' or 'Narcissus': both were known for their beauty, but both died through rejecting others and living for themselves alone. The tragedy may also be rooted in emotion rather than ambition. Basil's confession reveals a gap between his feelings and those of Dorian: on his side obsession, inspiration and longing, on his friend's only casual affection. By deferring Dorian's arrival, the text builds up **suspense**, but we may already be expecting that this relationship will have a painful outcome.

Lord Henry appears detached. Comments such as 'being natural is simply a pose, and the most irritating pose I know' (p. 7) provide a refreshingly witty contrast to the earnest Basil. They offer a new viewpoint on the theme of artifice versus nature and widen the discussion into the area of social hypocrisy. However, there is an extraordinary bond between the two friends: Lord Henry 'felt as if

**CONTEXT**

Edward Said's 1978 book *Orientalism* describes a tradition, both academic and artistic, of Western understanding of the East – often patronising or reductive – and how this was shaped by European imperialism in the eighteenth and nineteenth centuries. Throughout *Dorian Gray* you will find images of the East as a place of decadence and luxury.

**CONTEXT**

Lord Henry's remark 'I don't suppose that ten per cent of the proletariat live correctly' (p. 11) originally read 'live with their wives' (Norton Edition, p. 179), but this was changed by the *Lippincott's* editor, rather blunting the analogy with Henry's own marital habits.

he could hear Basil Hallward's heart beating' (p. 8). Perhaps Lord Henry's 'self-conscious and satisfied air' (p. 13) may also be vulnerable to change.

---

## GLOSSARY

| 5 | **laburnum** tree with dangling bright yellow flowers |
|---|---|
| | **tussore** raw unbleached silk |
| | **bourdon note** low rumbling note made by the bass stop of the organ |
| 9 | **Stars and Garters** that is, people entitled to the trappings of knighthood |
| 10 | *précis* summary |
| | **salon** place noted for the quality of its conversation |
| 11 | **Antinoüs** youth beloved of the Emperor Hadrian (see Chapter 9) |
| 12 | **Agnew** art dealer Sir William Agnew (1825–1910) |

---

## Chapter 2

- Basil wants Lord Henry to leave, but Dorian persuades him to stay while he sits for the portrait.
- Lord Henry talks to Dorian about the pursuit of pleasure and tells him that his youth and beauty are precious.
- Looking at the finished picture, Dorian wishes it could grow old in his place, saying that he would give his soul for that.
- Dorian chooses to go to the theatre with Lord Henry rather than dine with Basil.

**CHECK THE BOOK**

In the 1890 edition Basil is more open about his emotions: 'I couldn't be happy if I didn't see him every day. Of course sometimes it is only for a few minutes. But a few minutes with somebody one worships mean a great deal' (Norton Edition, p. 179).

Dorian is seen for the first time, sulky at the prospect of posing. Introduced to Lord Henry, he shares a joke with him about a mutual acquaintance, Lord Henry's Aunt Agatha. Basil asks Lord Henry to leave, but Dorian refuses to continue without him so Basil reluctantly invites his friend to stay, warning Dorian about his 'bad influence' (p. 17). Lord Henry refuses to accept the idea that any influence can be good, claiming that people lack the courage to live out all their inherent possibilities. He suggests that the wilful repression of bodily desire is damaging to the self. Dorian is drawn to this idea, but disturbed, and he hurries into the garden for fresh air. Intrigued by the effect of his words, Lord Henry follows. To Dorian's increasing fascination, Lord Henry proclaims the value of youth and beauty and urges Dorian to explore 'the wonderful life that is in you' (p. 21) while it is still possible.

When the portrait is complete, Dorian becomes resentful that he will age while it remains beautiful, saying that he would give his soul to reverse the situation. This jealousy of his own image leads him to snap at Basil and throw himself down 'as though he was praying' (p. 25). Basil accuses Lord Henry of making trouble and attempts to destroy the canvas. Dorian stops him and refuses to allow Lord Henry to buy the picture. Basil says it belonged to Dorian 'before it existed' (p. 26).

The situation cools over tea. Lord Henry invites Dorian to the theatre, and Basil asks Dorian to dine with him. Dorian chooses Lord Henry. As the chapter closes, Basil is wearing a 'look of pain' (p. 27).

## COMMENTARY

Our first glimpse of Dorian shows him with his back turned, as if, like Basil, the text is reluctant to allow us to meet him. We are already aware of other people's images of Dorian – Basil's inspiration; the 'ivory and rose-leaves' (p. 6) admired by Lord Henry; even the 'creature with spectacles and lank hair' (p. 14) that Lord Henry imagines from his conversation with Aunt Agatha – so we will be wondering what he is really like. But Dorian will always be bound up with his picture and its fate, and the text ensures that we see the portrait before the original. For the first time, too, we read that the portrait is 'life-size' (p. 16). It lodges itself in the imagination with a shock as we realise how closely it mirrors its subject.

In this chapter different kinds of force are brought to bear on Dorian, and the first is personal. As Basil plies his trade, Lord

**CHECK THE POEM**
William Blake's poem 'The Garden of Love' from *Songs of Experience* (1794) describes the destruction of true innocence through repression of natural impulses, in a world where 'Priests in black gowns were walking their rounds / And binding with briars my joys and desires.'

**CHECK THE BOOK**

One of the most popular novels of the period, George Du Maurier's *Trilby* (1894), is also set in the art world and tells the story of a young woman who has a beautiful voice but is tone-deaf. Hypnotised by her sinister mentor Svengali she becomes a great soprano, but when he dies her talent disappears. However, when confronted by his portrait, she falls into a trance and sings one last glorious burst of music.

Henry chats with Dorian as one aristocrat to another, demonstrating their shared access to certain circles as of right, in contrast to Basil's status as tolerated outsider. This may be what provokes the sulkiness in Basil that Dorian complains of.

The sharply observed exchange over Lord Henry's decision to stay prefigures Wilde the comic dramatist. Basil makes it plain he does not want him there, with what seems, on the surface, a friendly joke about Dorian's 'whims' being 'law' (p. 17). But Lord Henry understands Basil's true feelings. His remark 'you are very pressing' (p. 17) teeters on the edge of sarcasm and his excuse is transparently fictitious, its purpose being to compel Basil to give his reluctant invitation more warmly. Beneath the mask of good manners the two young men are discreetly struggling for Dorian's favour.

Having won this round, Lord Henry exerts a different kind of force and advances an argument that will be crucial for Dorian: the idea that 'to realise one's nature perfectly' (p. 18), even by giving in to temptation, is the highest duty to the self. On one level this is an argument about life and art. This view is essentially that of Walter Pater, who taught Wilde at Oxford. It effectively contradicts Basil, who in Chapter 1 implied that his world would manage to combine the era's two prevailing views about the nature and role of art (see **Literary background: The English Aesthetics**).

The idea of pursuing self-fulfilment should not in itself be taken to imply that Lord Henry is a corrupting influence. However, his rhythmic delivery adds another dimension: 'You, Mr Gray, you yourself, with your rose-red youth and your rose-white boyhood, you have had passions…' (p. 18). This is incantation rather than argument, a spell to induce a trance. Mesmerism, as hypnotism was then known, was in its infancy: it seems that Lord Henry can exercise power in more devious ways than by intellectual argument.

Another force comes into play as Lord Henry begins his praise of youth and beauty. The theme of *carpe diem*, or 'seize the day', features in poetry from ancient Rome onwards. It is a lover's argument: 'we will all grow old and die, so sleep with me while we are young enough to enjoy ourselves'. But if Lord Henry's tone is seductive, he does not get his way. Basil's entrance disrupts the mood and focuses Dorian's mind on the real object of his love – himself. 'The sense of his own beauty came on him like a revelation' (p. 23). Lord Henry's role has been that of the serpent in Eden who tempted Eve to eat the forbidden fruit. Afterwards, she and Adam realised that they were naked. Dorian's 'simple and … beautiful nature' (p. 15) has been transformed into a consciousness of his body and its power. He no longer sees his beauty as a gift but as something he must fight to retain at any cost.

After Dorian's wish there are several shifts in narrative tone. The most obvious is the movement into action with the near-fight over the painting, when Wilde establishes a resonant image that will recur: Dorian, Basil, the portrait and the knife. But there is also a new strand in the discussion of art and nature, a dispute over what constitutes the 'real' Dorian. The young man himself sees the picture as 'the shadow of his own loveliness' (p. 23). In his jealousy of the picture and his willingness to give his soul to look like it for ever, Dorian shows that he prefers shadow over substance. The phrase 'as though he was praying' (p. 25) a little later suggests the intensity of that desire.

For Basil, 'the real Dorian' is the picture that reflects his beauty, but his comment 'at least you are like it in appearance' (p. 27) implies that he knows he has lost Dorian to Lord Henry and that the picture is 'real' in the sense that it is all he really has of Dorian. When Basil and Lord Henry resume their struggle over who will spend the evening with Dorian, it is no longer comic. Basil suffers, and Dorian knows it. Has the boy with the 'simple and … beautiful' (p. 15) nature gone for good?

 **CHECK THE POEM**

One of the best-known English poems on this theme is Robert Herrick's 'Gather Ye Rosebuds While Ye May', a song urging girls to 'Be not coy, but use your prime / And while ye may go marry', as otherwise they may lose their looks and never achieve it.

**CONTEXT**

Plato explored the relationship between reality and image in his famous Myth of the Cave. Men are confined to a cave, seated around a fire. On the walls they see flickering shadows cast by the world outside. These shadows are all they know of the splendour of the world, just as all we know of ultimate reality are the imperfect earthly copies of the true nature of things (see **Themes: Art**).

**GLOSSARY**

| 16 | Schumann's Forest Scenes  piano music by German Romantic composer Robert Schumann (1810–56) (see **Language and style**) |
|----|----|
| 17 | Orleans  a gentleman's club frequented by Wilde's enemy, the Marquess of Queensberry |
|    | *moue*  pout |

continued

**GLOSSARY**

| | |
|---|---|
| 22 | **Tyrian convolvulus** a species of plant with the common name Morning Glory |
| 24 | **Hermes** Greek messenger-god with winged feet |
| | **Faun** minor deity with goat's ears and feet |
| 26 | **White's** a gentleman's club |
| | **dress clothes** a black suit worn with a pleated white shirt and black or white bow tie depending on the formality of the occasion |
| 27 | **hansom** a hired cab, denoting that the rider does not have transport of his own |

## CHAPTER 3

- Lord Henry learns about Dorian's wayward mother and his brutal grandfather.
- He attends a dinner where Dorian is present, and shows off his wit.
- Dorian leaves with Lord Henry, though he has promised to visit Basil.

Lord Henry calls on his uncle, Lord Fermor, to enquire about Dorian's family. He learns that Dorian's mother, the beautiful Margaret Devereux, eloped with a penniless army officer. Her father, Lord Kelso, hired 'some Belgian brute' (p. 29) to force the man into a fatal duel, and his daughter, cooped up in the family mansion, died soon afterwards, leaving her son, Dorian, to be reared by the cruel Kelso.

The conversation turns to the marriage prospects of Lord Henry's elder brother, who is currently being pursued by a rich American. Later, Lord Henry and Dorian attend a dinner given by Lord Henry's Aunt Agatha. They discuss America and current social problems in England. The topic of youth is raised, and Lord Henry entertains the company with the theory that one should commit youthful follies in order to remain young. He delights them and receives an invitation to

**CHECK THE BOOK**

In the late 1880s Leopold II of Belgium persuaded the noted explorer H. M. Stanley to open up the ivory and rubber trades in the Congo Basin through a series of agreements that gave the local people no rights and led to a vicious system of slavery enforced by mercenaries. Joseph Conrad's 1902 novel *Heart of Darkness* is based on his own experience of the Congo in 1890.

stay with Mr Erskine, the most cultured man in the company – but his performance is really aimed at Dorian.

As Lord Henry leaves, Dorian asks to go with him, even though he has already promised to visit Basil.

## COMMENTARY

This chapter was the first of five that Wilde added to the 1891 edition. It situates Dorian and Lord Henry in their shared social context (Basil is notably absent). The opening reveals a major preoccupation of their class: the importance of breeding and of securing, through the right marriage, enough money to maintain themselves in luxury. Wilde would satirise this snobbery and greed in his **social comedies**, in most of which characters' antecedents are dissected and their finances assessed by a formidable old lady.

Here the tone is also satirical, especially the ambassador's notion that he is entitled to his post by 'his birth, his indolence, the good English of his despatches and his inordinate passion for pleasure' (p. 28). However, Wilde also explores heredity and its relationship to human **motivation**, a topic of interest in a world aware of Darwin (see **Historical background: New sciences**). Here are reasons to explain why Lord Henry and Dorian behave as they do, although it is for us to decide whether heredity leaves them free to act differently.

Lord Henry is a younger son. This means that his inheritance will be relatively small. His earlier remark, 'my elder brother won't die, and my younger brothers never seem to do anything else' (p. 10), could be seen as a throwaway witticism. However, he admits that he lives on credit, 'the capital of a younger son' (p. 29), and deals with the same tradesmen as his elder brother, Dartmoor, presumably hoping that Dartmoor will absorb his debts. In this he resembles a figure common in Jacobean tragedy, the **malcontent** with more brains than money (often because of his younger-son status), who makes mischief to satisfy a grudge against the world.

Dorian's background also suggests a common literary figure, the romantic orphan. Because a wife took the status of her husband, a

 **CHECK THE BOOK**

Esther Summerson, the **narrator** in Dickens's *Bleak House,* is the secret child of an aristocratic lady and a poor man who calls himself 'Nemo', or 'nobody'. Bullied by the aunt who fosters her, she is regularly told: 'Your mother is your disgrace … and you were hers.'

**CONTEXT**

The Civil Service opened to competitive examination in 1870, although the Foreign Office, staffed by the sons of the wealthy, was exempt. In 1882 Gilbert and Sullivan's 'fairy opera' *Iolanthe* mocked the consternation expressed by men like Henry's uncle at the prospect of middle-class men wielding such power.

well-born woman who married 'beneath' her – or, worse, formed a liaison out of wedlock – was vulnerable. An orphan of such a match could suffer greatly. It is not clear whether Dorian is legitimate: he has some money his grandfather has been unable to withhold. His looks and charm suggest that he may find the happy ending of a typical literary orphan.

However, Dorian shares the bloodline of the vicious Kelso – and also seems to have been raised in appalling loneliness. This may explain why he expresses few opinions. To his best friends he is a blank canvas, which Basil sees as an innocence to be preserved and Lord Henry as an opportunity to inscribe whatever he likes: 'He was a marvellous type … or could be fashioned into a marvellous type, at any rate' (p. 31). Lord Henry's meditation is significant in the light of his lecture to Dorian in Chapter 2 about the malignity of influence. Is Lord Henry deceiving himself, or enjoying his duplicity?

The aristocratic chatter recurring throughout the story provides a backdrop to the three major characters. It is comic, but also illuminates the world in which Lord Henry, Basil and Dorian move, and its keynote is stasis. From the dullest – Lord Henry's uncle insisting that exams are 'humbug' because 'if a man is a gentleman, he knows quite enough, and if he is not a gentleman, whatever he knows is bad for him' (p. 29) – to the brilliant Mr Erskine 'fallen … into bad habits of silence' (p. 32), everything the gentry says is geared to preserving the status quo. Their charity – playing the piano to the East End poor – is, as Lord Henry states, merely 'amusing the slaves' (p. 34). When Mr Erskine suggests that he put his ideas on paper, Lord Henry pushes the idea aside; even he has no interest in reaching out to the wider world.

## GLOSSARY

| | |
|---|---|
| 28 | **the Albany** a very exclusive address, the former home of the second son of George III, the Duke of York, and always referred to by those who live there simply as Albany, without the 'the' |
| | **Prim** Juan Prim y Prats, who masterminded the Spanish coup of 1866 that overthrew Queen Isabella II |
| 29 | **English Blue-book** report of a Royal Commission or Parliamentary Committee |
| 30 | **jarvies** hackney cab drivers |
| | **pork-packers** the phrase has political connotations – 'pork-barrel' politics involve the appropriating of government funds for specific local projects; it also suggests an undignified way to earn money, as opposed to merely inheriting it |
| 31 | **that the meanest flower might blow** a phrase designed to echo Wordsworth's poem 'Intimations of Immortality from Recollections of Early Childhood', about the loss of innocence and harmony with nature |
| 32 | **Buonarotti** the sculptor and painter Michelangelo (1475–1564) |
| 33 | **American dry-goods** textiles, clothes and other useful non-perishable items |

## CHAPTER 4

- Dorian visits Lord Henry, and meets his wife.
- He tells Lord Henry that he is in love with a brilliant young actress, Sibyl Vane.
- Dorian tells Lord Henry that he wants him and Basil to watch Sibyl perform.
- Lord Henry ponders this turn of events and considers it as part of an experiment on Dorian.

A month later Dorian calls on Lord Henry, and encounters Lord Henry's eccentric wife, Victoria. When Lord Henry finally arrives

**CHECK THE BOOK**

Michael Holroyd's *A Strange Eventful History* (2008) gives a vivid picture of the lives of actors and actresses during the period, focusing on Ellen Terry, the most noted British actress of her day. A good friend of Wilde's, she played most of the Shakespearean roles associated with Sibyl.

Victoria leaves, and Lord Henry speaks disparagingly of marriage. Dorian responds by telling him that he is in love with an actress, Sibyl Vane.

Dorian recounts his first sight of Sibyl playing Juliet at a shabby little theatre, and describes her wonderful talent for becoming the Shakespearean heroines she plays. Lord Henry cynically asks what his relationship with her is like. At first, Dorian tells Lord Henry, he was reluctant to meet her, but her manager insisted and he is delighted by her innocence: she has nicknamed him 'Prince Charming'. He plans to bring Sibyl to the West End stage and wants Basil and Lord Henry to come and watch her the next day.

Dorian asks Lord Henry to write to Basil, whom he has not seen for a week, and they briefly discuss the way that a great artist can be a bore. When Dorian has gone, Lord Henry meditates on what is happening to the young man. He considers that this love affair may be the result of his own influence on Dorian, and goes on to ponder the relationship between body and soul. He anticipates the effects the affair may have on Dorian. Later, a note arrives from Dorian announcing his engagement to Sibyl Vane.

## COMMENTARY

As in Chapter 2, Wilde 'poses' Dorian for our attention at the outset. We can tell that a change has taken place. Previously he was standing, like a polite, shy guest, at Basil's piano, leafing through music suggestive of pastoral innocence. Now he is 'reclining in a luxurious armchair' (p. 38) entirely at ease in Lord Henry's house, reading some risqué literature. Dorian's annoyance at Lord Henry's lateness begins a strand that runs throughout the novel: the 'formal monotonous ticking' of the clock (p. 38) is the first of many **allusions** to time that will make us aware of its passing.

So far, the languid atmosphere has resembled that of the first encounter between Dorian and Lord Henry, but Lady Wotton breaks it up with a comical shock. In clothes associated with 'rage' and 'tempest' (p. 38), she is the first element of untidiness to enter this picture of luxurious idleness. Lady Wotton's speech, too, has its

**QUESTION**

When he adapted the novel for the stage, the playwright John Osborne suggested his wife, Jill Bennett, for the role of Dorian. If you were re-telling this story for a modern audience, how would you present the figure of Dorian? Might his class, gender, race or occupation be different?

funny side. Her line about pianists – 'Even those that are born in England become foreigners after a time, don't they? It is so clever of them, and such a compliment to art' (p. 39) – could come from one of Wilde's **social comedies**.

We do not know whether this is conscious wit or silliness. Lord Henry's remarks about their mutual deceptions and the disappointments of marriage suggest the latter, yet her comment to Dorian – 'I know you quite well by your photographs. I think my husband has got seventeen of them' (p. 38) – is a sharp observation. In a story so preoccupied with the power of the image, it makes us ponder not only Lord Henry's motives but also what Lady Henry makes of them.

There is an awkward pause after Lord Henry's **aphorism** 'Nowadays people know the price of everything, and the value of nothing' (p. 39). It may be that the lady is not quick-witted enough to reply in kind or that Lord Henry hopes silence will drive her away, but perhaps in this pause his wife is thinking that he is incapable of knowing *her* value. She has certainly indicated that Lord Henry's point of view is not the only way of looking at the world.

Though Dorian seems uncomfortable with Lord Henry's conclusions on 'analysing women' (p. 40), his account of wandering London with a 'passion for sensations' (p. 41) suggests that he is an apt pupil. Dorian has become a *flâneur*, a figure frequently found in late nineteenth-century literature – a man of privilege who wanders the city streets as a cynical but scientific observer. Lord Henry's musings show that he, too, is an observer of life – but they also imply that rather than stopping at observation, he may actively intervene.

As the conversation continues Dorian's expressions of love grow increasingly ardent, ending with 'I worship her!' (p. 46), an extravagance that bears out Basil's description of him as a youthful innocent. There is, however, a new dash of cynicism: 'Ordinary women never appeal to one's imagination' (p. 43).

> **CONTEXT**
>
> The 1890 edition contains a lively comic vignette of Basil's hostess introducing him to 'Sir Humpty Dumpty – you know – Afghan frontier – Russian intrigues – very successful man – wife killed by an elephant – quite inconsolable – wants to marry a rich American widow – everybody does nowadays – hates Mr Gladstone – but very much interested in beetles' (Norton Edition, p. 178).

## GLOSSARY

| | |
|---|---|
| 38 | *Les Cent Nouvelles* collection of bawdy French stories (1462) |
| | **Margaret of Valois** wife of Henri IV of France (1553–1615), known as both scholar and libertine |
| | *Manon Lescaut* novel about a man's love for a faithless woman, by Abbé Prevost (1697–1763) |
| | *Lohengrin* opera by Richard Wagner (1813–83) |
| 39 | frangipanni perfume derived from jasmine |
| 40 | *Rouge* and *esprit* blusher and wit |
| 42 | *les grandpères ont toujours tort* our grandfathers are always wrong |
| | **low-comedian** in a theatre company, one actor would adopt a lower-class persona and specialise in vulgar jokes |
| 46 | **Philistine** uneducated or barbaric person; from the chief opponents of the Israelites in the Old Testament |
| 47 | **agate** semi-precious stone; indicates that Lord Henry's brown eyes are also hard |
| 48 | **Giordano Bruno** (1548–1600) Italian thinker burned for heresy |

**CONTEXT**

Adam Ant had a hit in 1981 with the song 'Prince Charming'. The accompanying video showed him posing before a mirror that reflected him as a variety of popular film heroes, including the silent movie star Rudolph Valentino and the young Clint Eastwood.

## CHAPTER 5

- Sibyl Vane tells her mother about Dorian, whom she knows as 'Prince Charming'.
- Sibyl's brother James, a sailor, prepares to leave for Australia, and warns her not to trust Dorian. James vows to kill Dorian if he harms her.
- James asks his mother whether she was married, and learns that he and Sibyl are illegitimate.

Sibyl Vane and her mother are discussing Sibyl's love for Dorian. Mrs Vane is inclined to be cautious, urging her to concentrate on acting, as the manager of the theatre, Mr Isaacs, has made them a large advance on her salary. Sibyl's brother James arrives; he is a sailor, preparing to go to Australia. Concerned at his mother's snobbish dislike of his profession and unrealistic hopes of a 'brilliant marriage' for her daughter (p. 53), he urges her to look after Sibyl.

Walking in the park, James warns his sister to be careful. Dorian passes by in a carriage. James is angry that he has failed to see the face of this man Sibyl knows only as 'Prince Charming', and vows to kill him if he hurts Sibyl.

Before he leaves, James asks his mother if she was married to his father. When she admits she was not, he is even more apprehensive that Sibyl's love of a 'highly connected' gentleman (p. 58) will also end badly.

## COMMENTARY

This is the second of the new chapters added in the 1891 edition. It introduces the only characters other than the three central figures whose thoughts we will learn through **free indirect speech** (see **Language and style**), and their perspectives are very different.

The Vanes are shaped in their different ways by two forces. The first is economic necessity, as the setting, with its 'shrill intrusive light' (p. 50) and its single chair, in contrast to the opulent interiors described so far, makes clear. The second is theatricality. The **imagery** associated with Sibyl suggests that as an actress she has a complex relationship with her body and nature. She responds to the physical world but also responds physically to what she conjures up in her imagination. 'A rose shook in her blood, and shadowed her cheeks … . She had sent her soul to search for him, and it had brought him back. His kiss burned again upon her mouth. Her eyelids were warm with his breath' (p. 50). She is living out a romance she has created for herself, in which issues of class and money have no part.

In contrast, Mrs Vane's views are constructed by economic hardship and popular entertainment. She is always aware of money: the advance from Mr Isaacs would be worth over £30,000 by present standards, suggesting that she must be a shrewd negotiator (or perhaps that she intends to prostitute Sibyl to him).

> **CONTEXT**
>
> The Italian actress Eleonora Duse (1858–1924) had astounded London with the realism of her acting. Like Sibyl, she could produce bodily reactions such as blushing through the force of her imagination.

However, she is so saturated in what Wilde perceives as false stage conventions that she cannot respond authentically to people. She cannot simply embrace Sibyl once James has arrived, but turns the situation into a **tableau**, a theatrical image of mother and child for him to admire. This mixture of the mercenary and the **melodramatic** suggests that Mrs Vane will all too easily delude herself that Sibyl has a chance of social mobility: she imagines that Sibyl can raise herself by marriage, because the melodramas in which she earns her living have happy endings.

James perceives himself as injecting a note of realism. His choice of profession is not simply a rejection of his mother's social ambitions for him but the deliberate assumption of a working-class rather than a bourgeois identity. Ironically, even though James dislikes the theatre, the young sailor is a standard character of melodrama, a heroic representative of the working class set against a corrupt aristocracy.

This complex mixture of motives and perceptions in the Vane family contrasts with Dorian's simplistic account of his romance with Sibyl in the previous chapter. Wilde locates them with great precision in the Euston Road, a seedy area that nevertheless had a foothold in respectability. When James and Sibyl enter Dorian's territory, Hyde Park, they do so as tourists, not as of right. It is not surprising, but still disturbing, that Dorian can ride past the love of his life without noticing her.

The sense of foreboding is deepened with Mrs Vane's admission that both her children are illegitimate. The moment of honesty – even 'vulgar directness' (p. 58) – which temporarily shatters any attempt to cast a romantic glow on the situation, indicates the real emotional price Sibyl would pay if Dorian were to betray her. The speed with which Mrs Vane finds a new melodramatic **cliché** to perform, that of the 'desolate' mother saying farewell to her child (p. 59), makes it clear that Sibyl will find no emotional support if it happens.

GLOSSARY

| 50 | bismuth whitening powder used in stage make-up |
| | Prince Charming the man who recognises the true worth of Cinderella, with whom Sibyl evidently identifies herself |
| 53 | gallery the cheapest seats in the theatre, and the furthest from the stage; to 'play to the gallery' is to over-act |
| 54 | bushrangers Australian outlaws |
| 55 | hunting-crop light whip carried on horseback |
| 56 | orris-root powdered iris root used in making perfume |
| | victoria ... four-in-hand carriages; Dorian's is lighter and thus obscured by the Duke's, which requires four horses. |
| 57 | omnibus horse-drawn ancestor of the bus; the word means 'for everyone' |

**CHECK THE BOOK**

Perhaps the most famous melodrama with a nautical hero is Douglas Jerrold's *Black-Eyed Susan* (1829), in which a young sailor defends his fiancée from a smuggler and then from the lustful advances of his own captain. He is nearly hanged for this act of mutiny, but all ends happily. You can read this and a selection of other popular melodramas in George Rowell's *Nineteenth Century Plays* (1972).

## CHAPTER 6

- The friends discuss Dorian's engagement. Basil is worried; Lord Henry views it as a social experiment.
- They discuss Lord Henry's theory of pleasure.
- Lord Henry and Dorian set off together for the theatre, leaving Basil to follow.

Basil and Lord Henry are waiting for Dorian to join them at dinner. Lord Henry tells Basil about the engagement. Basil is horrified that Dorian is marrying 'beneath him' (p. 60). Lord Henry refuses to take a stand on the matter but feels that to be married and then desert his wife will make Dorian a 'wonderful study' (p. 61). Basil refuses to take this sentiment seriously.

Dorian arrives and describes how he proposed to Sibyl after her performance as Rosalind. Lord Henry sceptically gets him to admit that Sibyl was the first to raise the subject of marriage, and Dorian tells him that Sibyl has made him forget all Lord Henry's teaching.

**CONTEXT**

A performance of Shakespeare's *As You Like It*, in which the cross-dressing heroine of *Mademoiselle de Maupin* plays the cross-dressing Rosalind, is central to the romantic plot of Gautier's novel, and the description of Sibyl's costume has some echoes of the one its central character wears on stage.

**CONTEXT**

The image of Sibyl as a 'narcissus' echoes Lord Henry's praise of Dorian in Chapter 1. Narcissus, rejecting the love of all others, including the nymph Echo, was transformed into a white flower after dying of love for his own image in a pool. This is one of several ironic links between Sibyl and Dorian.

The three men discuss pleasure, and Lord Henry advances his theory of Individualism as the highest form of morality.

Dorian promises them that Sibyl's performance will demonstrate a new kind of ideal, and they leave for the theatre. Dorian and Lord Henry travel in Lord Henry's two-seater carriage. Basil follows in a hansom cab, feeling bereft.

## COMMENTARY

This chapter does little to advance the plot, but throws some light on the three central characters. The intervening chapter has created suspense as to how Basil will react to Dorian's engagement. By allowing Lord Henry, not Dorian, to break the news, the text shows Lord Henry's willingness to torture Basil.

Basil's feelings are more difficult to read. His entrance, cheerfully disparaging the government as not worth painting, suggests the Bohemian figure of Chapter 1. However, his remark about 'Dorian's birth, and position, and wealth' (p. 60) as barriers to the marriage suggests the exact opposite. Does he mean it, or is he trying to mask his personal pain at losing the young man he idolises?

Dorian's love for Sibyl seems rooted in her ability to inhabit more than one personality: 'I have had the arms of Rosalind about me, and kissed Juliet on the mouth' (p. 63). This suggests that he may unconsciously have chosen the female counterpart of himself. His own identity is blurring, and he echoes aspects of his friends.

Basil's feelings for him find an echo in Dorian's concern to protect Sibyl's innocence: 'the man who could wrong her would be a beast, a beast without a heart' (p. 63). His account of their kiss – 'my life had been narrowed to one perfect point of rose-coloured joy' (p. 62) – echoes Lord Henry's frequent comparisons of Dorian himself to a rose in Chapter 2 (p. 18). However, Lord Henry's remark to Basil that 'the only things that one can use in fiction are the things that one has ceased to use in fact' (p. 64) adds an ominous note to Dorian's delight in finding 'my wife in Shakespeare's plays' (p. 63). It suggests that unconsciously Dorian is living through her, just as Lord Henry hopes to live a 'fiery-coloured life' (p. 49) through Dorian.

Significantly it is at the engagement dinner that we see Dorian smoking for the first time: 'the perfect type of a perfect pleasure' (p. 65), customary with Lord Henry. As the dinner ends, Lord Henry manages to isolate Basil from Dorian for a third time. We get our first insight into Basil's feelings about the engagement – but does the 'sense of loss' (p. 65) spring from the projected marriage, or from the changes taking place in Dorian? We are left with the vivid image of Basil's lonely journey in the hansom.

---

### GLOSSARY

| | |
|---|---|
| 61 | Messalina (c. AD 25–48) wife of the Emperor Claudius, notorious for the number of her lovers |
| 62 | Tanagra figurine  small statue of red clay like those discovered in the ancient city in Beotia |
| | of age  twenty-one, the age at which one could marry without the consent of a parent or guardian |
| 65 | *fine-champagne*  brandy liqueur |
| | brougham  a luxuriously appointed closed carriage, often built to hold four |

---

### CHAPTER 7

- Sibyl plays Juliet very badly. Basil and Lord Henry leave after the second act.
- Dorian reproaches Sibyl, who explains that now she understands real love she cannot act any longer.
- He rejects her unkindly.
- At home, Dorian discovers a cruel expression on the face of his portrait. He resolves to end his friendship with Lord Henry.

Lord Henry, Dorian and Basil arrive at the shabby theatre. While Lord Henry is sceptical, Basil now says that he approves of the marriage in the light of Sibyl's effect on Dorian.

**CONTEXT**

Wilde uses this image of a predatory older man encouraging a younger one to smoke in Act III of his **comedy** *A Woman of No Importance.* In the play Gerald, who resembles Dorian in his youth and naiveté, is encouraged to smoke by the witty and cynical Lord Illingworth, who is secretly his father and wants to lure him away from his mother.

As the play begins Sibyl's Juliet seems wooden, and by the end of the second act the audience is hissing the performance. Lord Henry urges the friends to leave. Basil suggests that Sibyl is unwell. Grimly, Dorian dismisses Lord Henry and Basil and watches the end of the play.

Afterwards, in a rage, he visits Sibyl in her dressing-room. She is happy: she explains that she used to believe the fictions she was playing, but now that she has discovered the reality of love she hates the theatre and wants only to be with him. Dorian tells her she has killed his love and he leaves, ignoring her promises to do better. He says he will never see her again.

Arriving home, Dorian sees a new, cruel expression on the face of his portrait. He recalls his wish that it would change while he kept his youth and beauty. Troubled, he resolves to end his friendship with Lord Henry and make amends to Sibyl.

## COMMENTARY

This chapter develops the theme of art and reality and also throws light on the nineteenth-century doctrine of 'Separate Spheres' of activity for the sexes. The Victorian ideal of womanhood involved stability. Man might go out into the world and engage with work and ideas. Woman was meant to provide a core of spirituality, love and constancy in the home. The actress, endlessly adopting new identities, seemed to undermine this doctrine.

Ellen Terry, the most talented player of her generation, gave up the stage when she married, and her family – a noted theatrical dynasty – disapproved when she resumed acting after the marriage collapsed. Kerry Powell notes in his article on Wilde and actresses, 'A Verdict of Death' (*The Cambridge Companion to Oscar Wilde*, ed. Peter Raby, 1997), that in Victorian fiction the actress was a tragic figure, torn between domesticity and a career. However, Sibyl differs from her fictional counterparts in being abandoned because she *loses* the ability to shift identities. Dorian is unusual in delighting in Sibyl's self-transformations.

**CONTEXT**

Wilde's lifelong friend Mrs Bernard Beere, who scored a personal triumph in Wilde's *A Woman of No Importance*, wrote a story for Clement Scott's 1880 anthology *The Green Room* called 'The Tale of a Peacock', in which an actress is abandoned by her lover just before she goes on stage to play Ophelia. Her performance is brilliant, but as the character goes mad, so does she, and she is carried out of the theatre in a state of collapse.

The discussion of acting continues the implied debate on art in Chapter 2 (see **Themes: Art**). Lord Henry, sticking to the practical aspect of the situation, sees Sibyl's talent as irrelevant, assuming that Dorian will not let his wife work. Basil is clear that 'Love is a more wonderful thing than Art' (p. 69). Sibyl's position is more radical: she feels love and art cannot co-exist. The end of the chapter, however, suggests that the relationship between art and reality is more complex than the characters realise.

Wilde introduces the supernatural with careful slowness. As we come to accept that the change in the portrait is magical, not a figment of Dorian's guilty imagination, we are also considering the portrait's effect on Dorian. It is at once a reproach and a temptation to sin, and is more interesting to him than Sibyl. In Chapter 1 Basil compared meeting Dorian to finding a new medium, such as oil paint. Ironically, it seems that he *has* found a new medium, an art form capable of interacting with its subject. Dorian may end his day on an optimistic note, but a reader familiar with stories about supernatural bargains knows they never work out well.

 **CHECK THE POEM**

Sibyl's comment 'I have grown sick of shadows' (p. 70) echoes Tennyson's 'Lady of Shalott'. This poem of 1842 tells the story of a woman under a curse, who must spend her life weaving a web that shows images of a world that she can only see in a mirror. When Sir Lancelot rides past on his way to Camelot, she leaves her loom to look at him through the window. The mirror shatters, and she journeys down the river towards Camelot, but dies before reaching it. Lancelot's comment on seeing her body, 'She has a lovely face', suggests that he, like Dorian, does not have much idea that women are capable of complex responses to their situation.

| GLOSSARY | |
|---|---|
| 66 | Miranda  the daughter of Prospero in *The Tempest* |
| 67 | Good pilgrim ...  the first meeting of Romeo and Juliet in Act I of the play |
| | balcony scene  love scene between Romeo and Juliet in Act II, the best-known scene of the play |
| 72 | portico  gateway modelled on a classical arch, still to be seen in Covent Garden |
| | pure opal  the opal is a stone whose colours shift and change, and it is supposed to be unlucky |
| | nacre  mother-of-pearl |
| | Doge's barge  ceremonial vessel of the chief magistrate of the Republic of Venice |
| 73 | cupids  generally depicted as small winged children; Cupid is the god of love |

## CHAPTER 8

- Dorian looks at his picture again. Feeling guilty, he decides to write to Sibyl asking forgiveness and renewing his offer of marriage.
- Lord Henry arrives to tell him that Sibyl has killed herself.
- He persuades Dorian not to reproach himself, and Dorian comes to see Sibyl's death as a beautiful romance.
- Dorian decides that he will take advantage of the picture's strange power and live as he pleases. He goes to the opera with Lord Henry.

**CONTEXT**

The playwrights mentioned by Lord Henry – John Webster (c.1580–1625), John Ford (1586–c.1640) and Cyril Tourneur (c.1575–1616) – were rarely performed in Wilde's time. Their violent scenes were considered too crude for performance, although their poetry was admired. Webster is a particularly ironic choice for Lord Henry here. In his tragedy *The White Devil*, a woman is killed by kissing a poisoned portrait of the man she loves.

Dorian wakes very late. He ignores a letter that has arrived from Lord Henry, takes a bath, has breakfast and steels himself to look at the picture. It still wears a cruel expression. Having decided that he must make amends to Sibyl, Dorian writes a long letter asking her forgiveness.

Lord Henry arrives just as he has finished, and Dorian tells him that he intends to marry Sibyl. Lord Henry breaks the news that Sibyl is dead, having swallowed poison. He urges Dorian to go to the opera with him that evening. Although shocked at Sibyl's death, Dorian is aware that he does not feel grief. Lord Henry suggests that Dorian should think of the episode as if it were a play, and remarks that Sibyl was 'less real' than the characters she acted (p. 84). Dorian finds himself in agreement.

Alone again, Dorian considers his portrait and decides that he will have 'eternal youth, infinite passion, pleasures subtle and secret, wild joys and wilder sins' (p. 85) while the portrait bears the consequences. He goes to the opera.

## COMMENTARY

This chapter contains some barbed **satire** on Victorian attitudes to class and gender. Despite Dorian's good intentions of the previous night, nothing comes between the young aristocrat and his creature comforts. Wilde surrounds him with consumer luxuries (not all paid for) and several courses to eat for breakfast. Those who work for a living – like the valet and Sibyl herself – are either absent or too discreet to question his priorities.

While Lord Henry's witticisms might suggest that he does not share the blinkered attitudes of his own class ('one should never make one's *début* with a scandal. One should reserve that to give an interest to one's old age', p. 79), his practicality is chilling: 'I suppose they don't know your name at the theatre? If they don't, it is all right' (p. 79). Evidently he not only considers the aristocracy to be above the law but expects Dorian to share this view (which he does).

In Chapter 2 Dorian resented mattering less to Basil than 'your ivory Hermes or your silver Faun' (p. 24). Now he turns Sibyl into 'a wonderful tragic figure, sent onto the world's stage to show the supreme reality of Love' (p. 85). There is a savage **irony** in this **metaphor** of the theatre. The first person to use it in the novel is Basil, in Chapter 1, where he implies that the gifted, like Dorian, Lord Henry and himself, are superior to those who 'sit at their ease and gape at the play' (p. 7). Presumably, however, the gapers are aware that the 'play' of life involves genuine pain.

Lord Henry and Dorian 'gape' at Sibyl like a commodity. They also reveal themselves as full-blown adherents of the 'Separate Spheres' doctrine. Lord Henry even avers that women 'love being dominated' (p. 83). This comes as a shock: even if one has not always endorsed Lord Henry's point of view, he has seemed incapable of **cliché**.

Dorian too assumes the Separate Spheres division between male activism and feminine spirituality. Telling himself that he will marry Sibyl, without love, to atone for his cruelty, he is formulating a use for her – to 'keep me straight' (p. 81) in the face of the temptations the portrait offers. She is evidently to be the spiritual guardian of his home, the role imposed on women by the most conservative opponents of female emancipation.

 **CHECK THE POEM**

Of relevance to the 'Separate Spheres' debate are these lines from Canto VI of Lord Byron's long narrative poem *Don Juan*: 'Man's love is of man's life a thing apart, / 'Tis woman's whole existence …'. Although the prevailing tone of the poem is comic and even farcical, it was taken as a satisfactory summary of the emotional difference between the sexes.

## CONTEXT

In Shakespeare's play, Othello is deceived into thinking that his wife Desdemona (the daughter of Brabantio) is unfaithful, and he strangles her. His cry 'The pity of it!' is a sign of his delusion and self-pity, an ironic quotation for Dorian to think of here.

Dorian's comment that Sibyl's rejection of this role – her suicide – was 'selfish' (p. 81) is the darkest **irony** of the chapter. As he makes his 'choice' (p. 85), he sees the picture in the sentimental way that he sees the death of Sibyl. He ponders its future ugliness in the words 'The pity of it! the pity of it!' (p. 85), quoting Shakespeare's *Othello*, and thus linking his own fate to Lord Henry's comment: 'Cry out against Heaven because the daughter of Brabantio died. But don't waste your tears over Sibyl Vane' (p. 84). Dorian is already becoming cut off from his soul, treating it as a work of art.

## GLOSSARY

| | |
|---|---|
| 76 | **Sèvres china** porcelain from the famous factory near Paris founded in 1756 |
| | **Louis-Quinze toilet-set** hairbrushes, shaving gear and so on, from the time of Louis XV |
| 80 | **Patti** Adelina Patti (1843–1919), British-born soprano at the height of her fame at this period |
| 81 | **gold-latten** mixed metal containing brass; that is, Lord Henry is not 'real gold' |
| 82 | **sow poppies** for opium, the drug of forgetfulness |
| | **asphodel** lilies that were said to cover the Elysian Fields, the home of the dead in Greek mythology |
| 83 | **Imogen** heroine of Shakespeare's *Cymbeline*, a faithful wife |

## CHAPTER 9

- Basil visits Dorian, and is shocked that he is not grieving for Sibyl.
- He tells Dorian that he wants to exhibit the portrait, and tries to look at it.
- Basil mentions that the picture has a strange quality, and prompted by Dorian he confesses his love.
- Dorian says that he will never sit for Basil again, and resolves to hide the picture.

The next morning Basil arrives. When he called the day before to offer his condolences, he had refused to believe the servants who told him that Dorian was at the opera. He now reproaches Dorian for a callousness he attributes to Lord Henry's influence. Dorian tells him that he has come to see Sibyl's suicide as 'art' (p. 88), and also that he has grown up and changed. He asks Basil to remain his friend. Basil asks about the inquest, and Dorian makes it clear that none of the Vanes knew his surname.

Basil asks Dorian to sit for him again, but Dorian refuses, becoming distressed when Basil tries to look at the portrait and horrified by Basil's announcement that he intends to exhibit it. He questions Basil about his original unwillingness to do so. Basil inquires whether Dorian has noticed anything strange about the picture, frightening Dorian further.

Basil goes on to confess his adoration for Dorian and the powerful influence Dorian has had on his work. Dorian is disappointed. He tells Basil that he will remain his friend, but that he will never sit for him again. When Basil leaves, Dorian resolves to hide the picture where no one will ever see it.

## COMMENTARY

This is the first time that we see this pair of the central trio alone together. The interview between Basil and Dorian balances the

**CHECK THE FILM**

In Robert Zemeckis's 1992 comic film *Death Becomes Her*, a scientist (Bruce Willis) creates a potion that gives eternal life. His wife and his mistress (Meryl Streep and Goldie Hawn) both take it, but find that they have to deal with bullet holes, decay and other bodily problems. They order him to take the potion so he can use his skills to maintain their looks, but he cannot face the tedium of eternal life.

**CONTEXT**

The Emperor Hadrian had a young Greek lover named Antinoüs, many images of whom survived to provide an image of male beauty to later generations. He fell into the Nile while travelling in the Emperor's barge in AD132, causing Hadrian to go into a serious depression for eight years. Officially Antinoüs's death was an accident, although some thought it was murder, some considered it the suicide of a young man who knew that he would eventually lose his power along with his looks, and others suggested that he was making a ritual sacrifice, to restore the Nile floods after a period of drought. Dorian is compared to him more than once, and the overtones of violence in the story are no coincidence.

previous chapter, where Lord Henry persuades Dorian not to regret the death of Sibyl.

The same symmetry occurs in most treatments of the Faust story, including Marlowe's, where the man who sold his soul is visited by both Good and Bad Angels. As Dorian goes increasingly astray, Basil will act as Good Angel, balancing Lord Henry's advice and uttering moral warnings. However, as with all such stories, the Bad Angel can provide pleasures while the Good Angel can merely offer the consciousness of doing right.

Dorian's speech has become strongly reminiscent of Lord Henry's. The flippancy of 'There is a son, a charming fellow, I believe … a sailor, or something' (p. 87) is unlike anything we have heard from him so far. At the same time he insists 'I was a schoolboy when you knew me. I am a man now' (p. 89). It is children, rather than adults, who say how grown up they are.

Dorian is like a child dressing up as Lord Henry; he is also childishly afraid of hearing the details of Sibyl's inquest. At another level, he is plainly acquiring knowledge, speaking with self-assurance about 'old brocades, green bronzes, lacquer-work' (p. 89). Is perpetual youth going to enlarge Dorian's experience but leave him with the emotional equipment of a damaged child?

Basil's declaration of love was originally more explicitly homosexual and also charged with guilt. In Wilde's manuscript he asks if something in the picture has 'filled you perhaps with a sense of shame?'– a line Wilde deleted – and tells Dorian 'I have worshipped you with far more romance of feeling than a man should ever give to a friend' (a line Stoddart altered to 'usually gives') (Norton Edition, p. 232). In the 1891 text, Basil's desire for Dorian is still apparent, but less overt. This reticence, however, fits Basil's cautious nature. To be direct might invite rejection and end the relationship altogether.

Basil and Dorian understand Basil's love differently. Dorian finds Basil ridiculous with his 'absurd fits of jealousy, his wild devotion' (p. 94), but is primarily concerned with himself, wondering whether he will experience something similar. Basil is not ashamed of his love but analyses it as part of his understanding of the world as a whole. His sophisticated distinction between 'compliment' and 'confession' (p. 93) resembles Sibyl's articulate analysis of the collapse of her talent. However, their conclusions about love and art are different.

For Basil his breakthrough as an artist comes when he paints Dorian not costumed as a mythological or historical figure but as himself. Rather than destroying him as it did Sibyl, Reality has entered his art and transformed it. It is as if Dorian always provokes others to ponder a complex relationship between art and reality, shadow and substance, which he himself cannot grasp – perhaps because he is only a kind of shadow of his painted self.

This chapter might be described as the beginning of Dorian's real relationship with the picture. From now on, no human being will compete with it.

**CHECK THE BOOK**

Gyles Brandreth has written two novels in a series of Oscar Wilde Murder Mysteries, which show Wilde playing detective and often discussing a case with his friend Conan Doyle. *Oscar Wilde and the Candlelight Murders* was published by John Murray in 2006, and *Oscar Wilde and the Ring of Death* in 2008.

## GLOSSARY

| | |
|---|---|
| 85 | *Globe* evening newspaper, also read by Sherlock Holmes |
| 88 | **died as Juliet might have died** Juliet (played by Sibyl at her last performance) kills herself because she finds her faithful lover and husband dead beside her – not Sibyl's situation at all |
| 89 | *ennui* boredom |
| | *la consolation des arts* the consolation of the arts |
| | vellum fine leather |
| 91 | Rue de Sèze Georges Petit's gallery exhibited the work of the Impressionists |
| 92 | Adonis youth desired by Venus, killed by a boar |
| | Adrian's barge that is, the Emperor Hadrian |
| | turbid cloudy or muddy |
| 94 | panegyrics praises |

**CHECK THE NET**

The tapestry in Dorian's old schoolroom may well have inspired a short story by his friend Vernon Lee (b. Violet Paget, 1856–1935), 'Prince Alberic and the Snake Lady' (1896), about a boy who imagines himself in the world depicted on the tapestry in his room, and becomes obsessed in particular with its image of a beautiful woman. When he is sent to a real place just like that on the tapestry, he falls in love with the lady, who is really a serpent. You can read the story at **http://gaslight. mtroyal.ca** – find it under the 'Texts by Author' section.

## CHAPTER 10

- Dorian becomes afraid of what his servant Victor might know.
- He organises the removal of the picture to his old schoolroom.
- Depressed, Dorian settles down with a book from Lord Henry, which has a powerful effect on him.

Dorian begins to wonder if his servant Victor has seen the changed picture. He orders him to fetch some men from the frame-maker and demands from the housekeeper, Mrs Leaf, the key to the door of his abandoned schoolroom. Briefly, Dorian wishes that he had confided in Basil.

When the frame-maker arrives, Dorian dispatches Victor on another errand to get him out of the way. Victor is sent to Lord Henry with a note asking him for something for Dorian to read. The men carry the shrouded picture up to the attic.

When they have finished Dorian finds that a book has arrived from Lord Henry along with a newspaper cutting about Sibyl's inquest, increasing his concern about how much Victor might know. The book absorbs Dorian for hours. It tells the story of a young man who tries to live out all the passions the world has ever experienced. Fascinated by what he reads, Dorian is late for dinner with Lord Henry.

### COMMENTARY

In literature or in dreams, an upper room such as an attic is considered to symbolise an aspect of the psyche of which the everyday self is unaware. In the Gothic (see **Literary background: The Victorian Gothic**) and fairy tale traditions, such a room usually harbours a secret involving violence or disgrace. (*Jane Eyre* draws on this tradition when the mad wife of Jane's beloved Mr Rochester is revealed in her apartments at the top of Thornfield House.)

The room in Dorian's house had been 'specially built' (p. 98) by Lord Kelso for his grandson – evidently he saw Dorian himself as a shameful secret. The fact that the room has been untouched since Kelso died suggests that Dorian resents this – but, **ironically**, he treats the 'real' Dorian on the canvas in the same way, banishing it from his sight. In *Lippincott's* the character of the housekeeper, Mrs Leaf, is more developed, as a comic figure whose relationship with Dorian is loving and maternal. In this edition her role is purely functional. This underlines the theme of the chapter: isolation.

Throughout, Dorian strips himself of human contact. He decides it is 'too late' (p. 96) to patch it up with Basil. He is even too rapt in thought to talk to the frame-maker, comically failing to notice the transparent adoration of his assistant. Increasingly, Victor the servant becomes the object of near-paranoia: at the beginning of the chapter he is 'impassive' (p. 95), later he has 'treacherous eyes' (p. 96) and by the end he is 'a spy' (p. 99).

While the chapter offers a psychological basis for Dorian's behaviour – a lonely and unwanted child may well become self-obsessed – the theme of isolation is also sharply relevant to a world faced with the 'blackmailer's charter' (see **Historical background: Crime and punishment**). Dorian would not be the only man in 1891 to be afraid of 'some servant who had read a letter, or overheard a conversation, or picked up a card with an address' (p. 99).

Isolation is also an inevitable aspect of the **Faustian bargain**. An ageless being is cut off from people who grow old and die. Dorian's response to the report of Sibyl's inquest underlines this. He thinks of himself in the **third person**: 'What had Dorian Gray to do with Sibyl Vane's death? ... Dorian Gray had not killed her' (p. 100). This inability to connect with the 'horribly real' (p. 100) echoes the growing isolation of Faustus in Marlowe's play. And just as Mephistopheles the devil provides Faustus with entertainment, so Lord Henry sends Dorian a crucial book.

**CHECK THE BOOK**

A classic feminist text, Sandra Gilbert and Susan Gubar's *The Madwoman in the Attic: The Woman Writer and the Nineteenth-Century Literary Imagination* (1979), argues that the figure of the mad Mrs Rochester is an embodiment of the suppressed rage and energy of Jane Eyre herself.

**CONTEXT**

In Marlowe's *Doctor Faustus* (pub. *c.* 1589–92), the hero begins to contemplate repentance and the devil Mephistopheles offers him a pageant of the Seven Deadly Sins to 'delight his mind'. The book Lord Henry provides and the pleasures it inspires within the next chapter have something of the same function.

**GLOSSARY**

95  pall for the dead  a covering for a coffin, or sometimes for the corpse itself, used at a funeral

96  Montaigne ... Winckelmann  the French Renaissance essayist and thinker Montaigne (1533–92) and the German art historian Johann Winckelmann (1717–68)

texture  fabric

97  Fonthill  famous pseudo-Gothic mansion owned by the eccentric Gothic writer William Beckford (1760–1844)

98  *cassonne*  chest

unpictured sins  literally 'unimagined' but used here to imply that they have not yet affected the portrait

100  death by misadventure  suicide was a crime in the nineteenth century, and this phrase was used to allow the subject the benefit of the doubt

*argot*  slang, especially criminals' private language

## CHAPTER 11

- Dorian lives under the influence of the book.
- There are rumours that he is living an evil life, but his patronage of the arts makes him admired.
- Dorian explores perfumes, music, jewels and embroidery.
- He ponders his own sinister ancestry and the lives of wicked men of history.

Dorian spends years under the influence of the book Lord Henry has given him, keeping nine copies in special bindings to fit his moods. While the story of the pleasure-seeking Parisian seems to reflect his own, he does not share the disease and decay of the book's hero, as he remembers to his own delight.

There are rumours that Dorian is living an evil life, but his innocent face seems to refute this, and he shares with others his experience and knowledge of the arts and fashion in a way that makes him something of a cult hero. Intellectually, he links himself to both the Catholic Church and Darwinism. He also studies perfume, music, jewels and embroidery.

However, Dorian's relationship with the portrait is too important for him to leave England for long. He is also increasingly anxious that someone may see it. He ponders his own ancestry, and the family portraits that include some notorious figures including his wild young mother. He feels that their lives are also his, just as in one chapter of the novel Lord Henry gave him the hero shared the lives of the more notorious Roman emperors.

Dorian reads this chapter obsessively, and the next which describes the lives of murderous courtiers of past centuries. The book is acting as a poison, draining Dorian of moral sense.

## COMMENTARY

Wilde's novel is constructed with great care, and this chapter is his solution to a problem inherent in all stories of the devil's bargain:

 **CHECK THE NET**

Chapter 11 is so full of information that it can seem rather daunting. Wilde drew much of this from what later became the Victoria and Albert Museum. You can still find there some of the objects mentioned in the text; other exhibits will give you an idea of what the items in Dorian's collection might look like. You can conduct your own search for images by going to **www.vam. ac.uk** – go to 'Collections', then 'Search the collections' and type in the names of objects you would like to find.

## CONTEXT

Wilde's sources for this chapter include handbooks produced for the South Kensington Museum (now the Victoria and Albert Museum): Carl Engel's *Musical Instruments* and A. H. Church's *Precious Stones*. His work as editor of *Woman's World* proved useful too. He drew the information and some of the text on embroideries from Ernest Lefebure's *Embroidery and Lace: Their Manufacture and History from the Remotest Antiquity to the Present* (1888), which he reviewed in the November 1888 issue.

**QUESTION**

Choose any one object from Dorian's collection and find out all you can about it. What might it mean to him, or what might it symbolise for the reader?

once the soul has been sold, suspense disappears. The hero will not struggle to overcome the temptation to commit ordinary crimes, and will get away with them.

The energy of the plot has to come out of the possibility of repentance. To keep our interest in that possibility alive, the storyteller cannot allow the hero to revolt or disgust us so much that we do not want him to be saved. On the other hand, a damned soul must be guilty of some acts more terrible than people commit in crime stories, to keep the possibility of hell real.

Long life is part of the bargain, which leaves the problem of avoiding repetition. Wilde solves this by collapsing stories of notorious figures into Dorian's own. Dorian may only imagine living the life of Nero, who had Christians torn apart by wild beasts, or Caligula, who committed incest and murder (p. 115), and he does not consume the blood of young boys, like the notorious pope he reads about (p. 116). However, the reader associates him with this lived experience across the centuries.

Yet Dorian himself remains an **ambiguous** figure. The ugliness of the portrait proves he is not guiltless, but he also embodies wonderful possibilities. In his passion for art and science he imitates Leonardo da Vinci, as described by Walter Pater in *The Renaissance*. His study of the arts suggests both conspicuous consumption and a healthy concern for his own intellectual development. Some of the identities he tries out contain the possibility of social transformation.

The figure of the dandy, for instance, could be more than a fashion role model. Dandyism meant a commitment to personal originality and style, offering a way of weathering the collapse of the old social certainties with grace. Dorian's interest in Catholicism reflects a wider revival within England, especially at Oxford. However, Wilde adds a typically double-edged comment: 'he never fell into the error of arresting his intellectual development by any formal acceptance of creed or system' (p. 106). Is Dorian keeping an open mind, or merely going through the motions?

There is an entertaining paradox about this chapter. It may deal with sin and decadence, but it imparts a great deal of information that the interested reader could follow up with a trip to the South Kensington Museum (later the Victoria and Albert Museum). It has a solidly educational function that even Ruskin might have approved of.

## GLOSSARY

| | |
|---|---|
| 103 | Dante Dante Alighieri (1265–1321), Florentine poet and author of the *Divina Commedia*, an imaginary journey through heaven and hell |
| 104 | *arbiter elegantiarum* setter of fashion |
| 106 | *panis coelestis* literally 'holy bread', the communion wafer |
| | antinomianism belief that we are not bound by any moral law |
| | *Darwinismus* German version of evolutionary theory which sees the life of the individual as repeating that of the human race |
| 108 | Cortes conqueror of Mexico in 1519 |
| | *Tannhäuser* 1845 opera by Wagner on the subject of forgiveness |
| | *de la vieille roche* from the old rock, the finest turquoise |
| 109 | John the Priest mythical king usually called Prester John |
| | *parsemé* spangled |
| 110 | velarium awning |
| | *Madame, je suis tout joyeux* my lady, I am overjoyed |
| 112 | blackballed members of exclusive men's clubs would vote to admit or expel members by dropping a white (acceptance) or black (rejection) ball into a hat |
| 113 | coiners forgers, or people who clipped minute quantities of silver or gold from the coinage, reducing its value |
| 115 | *toedium vitoe* weariness of life |
| 116 | minion servant, slave, favourite |
| | gilded a boy to paint a living body with gold is to kill it by preventing the skin from breathing |

**CONTEXT**

The painting of Dorian's mother suggests a portrait by George Romney (1734–1802 ) of Emma Hamilton (1765–1815) as a Bacchante. Born into poverty, she married the British envoy at Naples and later became the mistress of Lord Nelson. In the *Bacchante* picture she portrays a follower of the god of wine; she wears a loose and revealing robe, her flowing hair is dressed with vine leaves and she carries a staff tipped with a new moon.

## CHAPTER 12

- Eighteen years later, Basil comes to see Dorian.
- Basil reproaches Dorian for the terrible rumours about his life, saying that he would have to see Dorian's soul to know the truth.
- Dorian says that he can show him his soul.

**CHECK THE BOOK**

The mysterious absence of Basil is a running joke in the graphic novel *The League of Extraordinary Gentlemen* by Alan Moore, Kevin O'Neill, Ben Dimagmaliw and Bill Oakley (2000) about a group of crime-fighting Victorian 'superheroes' from the works of Bram Stoker, Jules Verne, H. G. Wells and Rider Haggard. Works of art by the missing Basil decorate locations throughout.

It is the night before Dorian's thirty-eighth birthday. Coming home in the fog, he encounters Basil, who has just tried to visit him and given up waiting. Basil is planning to leave for Paris, but asks to stay for half an hour. He expresses concern at the rumours about Dorian that are rife in London society. He says that he has told a close friend whose wife's name is linked with Dorian's that Dorian is 'incapable' (p. 121) of such things, but points out that in order to know the truth he would have to see Dorian's soul. Dorian tells him that he can, and invites him upstairs.

## COMMENTARY

Wilde altered Dorian's age from thirty-two – a turning point in his own life, when he began his relationship with Robbie Ross – to thirty-eight. The turning point in Dorian's life is of a very different kind. Thirty-eight is in no sense 'old'. However, eighteen is the point at which a boy becomes a man, and Dorian has therefore lived out a whole second 'youth' since we last had a detailed account of his daily life eighteen years earlier.

While the previous chapter was concerned with historical figures and 'evil' as an abstract quality, this one is full of specific names. Although we do not know exactly what Dorian has done, these names root his acts in reality: their consequences are being experienced by people in a recognisable context. Dorian sneers at the hypocrisy of the middle class, although the codes that have been violated by the figures Basil has named are those of the aristocracy, as he must know perfectly well.

One name undermines Dorian's self-righteous bluster: that of Lord Henry's sister. Dorian met her for the first time the night after Sibyl Vane died. The smoothness of his transition from betraying a working woman to betraying an aristocratic one makes it hardly surprising that Basil refuses to accept any kind of argument based on class.

Meanwhile, Dorian seems to have discovered a new sin. He intends to use the portrait in order to make Basil suffer, a decision the text links specifically to the 'madness of pride' (p. 121), considered by the church to be the worst of all sins. He begins this torment with 'Don't touch me' (p. 121), underlining his rejection of Basil as lover or friend.

The thick fog in which Basil meets Dorian, the elaborate lie Dorian constructs to explain his change of servant (Victor's curiosity might have made him a useful witness) and the reference to Basil's habit of travelling light (implying that he is doing so incognito), are reminiscent of a Sherlock Holmes story. We may be about to learn something about the 'disappearance' of Basil that was mentioned in the first chapter.

**CONTEXT**

Possibly the oldest story ever written down is a tale of doubles, *The Epic of Gilgamesh*, preserved on twelve clay tablets in the library collection of the seventh-century BC Assyrian king Ashurbanipal. It revolves around the relationship between King Gilgamesh and his inseparable friend, Enkidu, who is half wild and undertakes dangerous quests with him. When Enkidu dies Gilgamesh searches for immortality, but he cannot bring back his friend.

**GLOSSARY**

| 118 | Gladstone bag a hinged suitcase, convenient for Basil to carry himself rather than requiring a porter |
| --- | --- |
| | Ulster a long, loose overcoat, which envelops the figure and would make the wearer difficult to recognise |
| | marqueterie wood inlaid to form a pattern |
| | *Anglomanie* passion for English things |
| | hock and seltzer white German wine with fizzy mineral water from Selters, in Prussia, Wilde's own favourite drink |
| 119 | the Dudley art collection of the Earl of Dudley, then in a gallery in Piccadilly |

## CHAPTER 13

- Dorian takes Basil to the attic, where he eventually recognises the picture.
- Basil urges Dorian to repent but, maddened with hatred, Dorian stabs him.
- Dorian hides Basil's belongings. He ensures that the servant will think that he has just arrived home.
- He looks for the address of a man who will help him.

Dorian leads Basil, who is half convinced that Dorian is 'mad ... or playing a part' (p. 123), to the room containing the picture. When Dorian draws the curtain the image is horrible, but Basil recognises the figure of Dorian in the portrait. Dorian reminds him of the wish that he made and Basil urges him to pray.

Seized by sudden hatred for Basil, Dorian picks up a knife and rushes at him, 'stabbing again and again' (p. 126). He then calms himself. He locks the door of the room and, stepping onto the balcony, checks that no one in the street below has overheard the struggle. Dorian attempts to leave the room without looking at the corpse, but outside the door realises that he has left the lamp behind. He returns to fetch it and cannot help 'seeing the dead thing' (p. 127).

Dorian hides Basil's belongings, then slips on his coat, goes outside and knocks on his own front door so that the servant will let him in and assume that he has just arrived home. He asks if anyone has called, and is told that Basil came but then went away. Dorian searches in the Blue Book for a name and address.

## COMMENTARY

The chapter reflects Wilde's interest in the Gothic novel (see **Literary background: The Victorian Gothic**). There are carefully established sound and lighting effects: 'the lamp cast fantastic shadows on the wall' and 'a rising wind made ... the windows rattle'

(p. 123); the picture furnishes a secret lair full of damp, decay and mildew, and the 'drip, drip, drip' of Basil's blood (p. 126) is loud enough to be heard as it falls on the carpet.

These Gothic terrors are, however, contained within a modern environment: Dorian kills just a few yards away from a London bobby on the beat, in a civilised urban landscape lit by gas lamps and traversed by hansom cabs. The contrast not only intensifies the horror but develops the Gothic genre. Rather than occurring in distant and exotic locations that provide imaginative escapism for the reader, the gore and decay are projections of Dorian's own mental state.

**CONTEXT**

Basil's exclamation on p. 125 was censored by *Lippincott's*, although it seems clear that it is more a prayer than a profanity.

Dorian tells Basil: 'Each of us has Heaven and Hell in him' (p. 125). Similarly, the devil Mephistopheles tells Marlowe's Faustus, who is puzzled that a damned soul can come to earth to tempt him, 'This is hell, nor am I out of it' (I. 3. 76). The echo of such a line, put by Marlowe into the mouth of a damned soul who cannot help speaking the truth, may well suggest the state of Dorian's own soul.

Basil talks about repentance, drawing tears from Dorian, but he is aware that the biblical language he is using is a relic of 'boyhood' (p. 125) rather than a living force. There seems to be no contemporary language adequate to Dorian's situation in a world where faith is waning.

**CHECK THE POEM**

Dorian echoes a passage many of Wilde's readers would know in Milton's *Paradise Lost*. Satan claims, as a ruler, the Hell to which he has been sent with the lines: 'The mind is its own place, and in itself / Can make a heaven of hell, a hell of heaven' (Book II, lines 254–5).

Dorian could be described as 'in hell', in that he is losing his sense of reality. The detachment with which he spoke of Sibyl's death is now apparent in his body as well as his voice. The emotion he shows is 'the passion of the spectator' (p. 124), while he is simultaneously an actor, smelling a flower 'or pretending to do so'. This phrase suggests that Dorian's speech blaming Basil for his fate, during which he dramatically crushes the flower, is a piece of self-conscious theatre. Dorian, at once actor and spectator, is whipping up Basil's self-reproach in order to enjoy the spectacle of his suffering.

Dorian may believe that his sudden hatred for Basil is 'whispered into his ear by those grinning lips' on the canvas (p. 125), but Wilde

Verse LXVI of Edward FitzGerald's 1859 translation of the Persian poem *The Rubaiyat of Omar Khayyam* (probably familiar to Basil with his love of oriental décor) reads: 'I sent my Soul through the Invisible, / Some letter of that After-life to spell: / And by and by my Soul return'd to me, / And answer'd "I Myself am Heav'n and Hell"'.

qualifies the suggestion with 'as though'. Dorian's acts may feel to him like performances, or as if they are not his own, but the text is clear about what has happened. Basil has become what psychologists term **abjected**, a process that makes it possible for people to treat individuals or even whole races with violence. Dorian has made Basil wretched by expressing contempt, rejection and blame. Now he hates Basil precisely because his resulting misery makes him seem less than human. Therefore Dorian treats him even more unkindly.

Dead, Basil is a 'thing … a dreadful wax image' (p. 127). If the name 'Basil Hallward' means anything to Dorian at the end of the chapter, it is as a figure in a story: 'Paris! Yes. It was to Paris that Basil had gone, and by the midnight train, as he had intended' (p. 127). That phrasing in the **pluperfect** tense makes the statement sound like a matter of fact, not to be disputed. It is as if Dorian himself believes his carefully constructed alibi.

**GLOSSARY**

124   vermilion red

satyr mythological figure, a man with the legs of a goat; satyrs were followers of the wine-god Bacchus and were noted for drunkenness and lust

126   iniquities sins

great vein that is behind the ear the jugular, the largest vein

127   arabesques geometrical shapes that suggest the forms of the natural world

red star the planet Mars, named after the god of war

128   Blue Book (different from that in Chapter 3) a list of the socially prominent

## CHAPTER 14

- Dorian begins his day at leisure and sends the servant with a note for Alan Campbell.
- When he begins to feel troubled, he reads the poetry of Gautier.
- Alan Campbell arrives and Dorian asks him to dispose of the body. He is reluctant, but Dorian shows him a letter which he will send if Alan refuses to help him.
- Five hours later, the body of Basil has gone.

Dorian sleeps until his valet wakens him. He fusses with his clothes and lingers over his food. He sends the servant to Alan Campbell, a man to whom he was previously close, with a letter. While Dorian waits for a reply, he reads poetry to distract himself. He becomes increasingly agitated. When Campbell arrives he is chilly towards Dorian, and says he has only agreed to see him as the letter called it 'a matter of life and death' (p. 133).

Dorian tells Campbell that there is a dead man upstairs, and that he wants him to dispose of the body. Campbell refuses. Dorian at first claims that the death was suicide, but then admits that he has committed murder and pleads with Campbell to save him from the gallows. When he still refuses, Dorian shows him a letter he has written which he threatens to send if Campbell does not co-operate. Campbell agrees, and Dorian sends the servant for the equipment Campbell needs.

When Dorian takes Alan to the attic where Basil is sitting dead in a chair, he remembers that the previous night he had for the first time forgotten to cover the picture. As he rushes to do so now, he sees 'a loathsome red dew that gleamed, red and glistening' on one of the portrait's hands, 'as though the canvas had sweated blood' (p. 138).

Campbell sends Dorian away and locks the attic door. Five hours later Campbell leaves the house, saying that they will never meet again. The body is gone.

**CONTEXT**

Theophile Gautier's (1811–72) *Enamels and Cameos* was published in 1852, while the writer was touring the Middle East. The volume was a watershed in that Gautier abandoned the Romantic approach, which attempted to engage the reader in a total emotional response, in favour of a focus on poetic form that gained its effects through carefully arranged sound patterns.

 **CHECK THE BOOK**

Some of the material here – the crocodiles, the way the drug affects the perception of time and space – is also found in Thomas De Quincey's 1821 *Confessions of an English Opium Eater*.

## CONTEXT

Two poems in *Enamels and Cameos* are meditations on hands: one on the sculpted hand of a woman, which Gautier imagines as made for love and beauty; the other on the mummified hand of Pierre François Lacenaire (1800–36), a French poet and murderer, which leads him to contemplate the consciousness of evil.

**WWW. CHECK THE NET**

Tintoretto (literally 'the little dyer'; real name Jacopo Comin, 1518–94) was one of the greatest Venetian painters of the Renaissance and made spectacular use of *chiaroscuro* (light and dark). You can view some of Tintoretto's paintings at **www. paintingdb.com** – find Tintoretto under 'T'.

## COMMENTARY

Wilde uses the same kind of symmetry here as in Chapters 2 and 4, in which Dorian is 'posed' to echo and contrast with a previous image of him. Here he lies peacefully asleep, as he does at the start of Chapter 8 following his betrayal of Sibyl. In each case Dorian has made a decision which will seriously affect his own personality.

In rejecting Sibyl, Dorian chose to identify with Lord Henry rather than with Basil and to value art over love, and the result was a new callousness in the portrait and in his own behaviour. Sibyl's suicide, though, was her responsibility: the murder of Basil is Dorian's. He is now, irrevocably, a killer. Dorian, and we, are in no doubt that the murder will have a profound effect on him. Dorian is clearly imagining himself as a Faustian hero who achieves 'strange triumphs' (p. 129) in pride, as if challenging God himself. Murder is 'a thing to be driven out of the mind' (p. 129), a threat to his convenience like an unwanted love-letter.

Wilde shows the damage to Dorian's psyche without overt moralising. Instead, he uses literary **allusion**. As Dorian tries to distract himself with poetry, the images reflect his inner landscape rather as a dream sequence in a film shows us what cannot be articulated. First comes a snatch of poetry about the hand of a murderer. As Dorian gazes at his own prettier hand, the reader is reminded of Lady Macbeth, walking in her sleep as she tries to wash away the blood that she dreams is on her hands. Shakespeare's tragedy is one of the first in literature to show a self making evil choices until the capacity to choose good is lost.

The images of Venice evoke Dorian's travels with Basil, who 'had gone wild over Tintoret' (p. 131). Tintoretto was a key painter for Ruskin: Basil appears here not only to haunt Dorian in his own right but to remind the reader of his Ruskinian view of art as a power to make people better. It is no surprise that the poem does not work as escapism for Dorian.

Finally, in Wilde's rather free translation of scraps of verse from Gautier's *What the Swallows Told*, some frightening images – predatory crocodiles and vultures (p. 131) – hint at visions of a kind to suggest that Dorian has a taste for opium. As Time itself seems to slow down, we could be reading an account of the drug's effects.

In contrast, the actual *action* of the chapter is narrated with brisk economy. The dialogue is simple, and depends on small details of the social code for much of its impact. Alan Campbell stubbornly keeps his hand in his pocket rather than shake Dorian's hand, but once the blackmailing letter is produced Dorian can touch him and know he will not be shaken off. Alan begins by addressing Dorian as 'Gray', then he becomes 'Dorian'; eventually Alan will not name him at all. While he expresses clear dislike and contempt, he uses no vulgar language or insulting epithets.

Dorian's whole survival strategy comes from his awareness of the hypocrisy of his world. Lord Henry once hoped that Dorian might become the figurehead of a 'new Hedonism' (p. 21) and defy its conventions. Instead, Dorian is simply exploiting them with criminal intent.

The ticking clock motif comes to the fore in this chapter. The clock seems to enter the minds of both Alan and Dorian, 'dividing Time into separate atoms of agony' (p. 136).

**CONTEXT**

The pressure Dorian is putting on Campbell can be gauged by a story about Wilde's model for Alan Campbell, the scientist Sir Peter Chalmers Mitchell. Wilde had been introduced to him in London and asked his advice on how to get rid of a body. Years later, when Wilde was living in exile, they found themselves in the same café in France. Mitchell's companions left when they saw Wilde, but Mitchell made a point of coming to sit with him. Wilde told him, 'I used you in *Dorian Gray*, but I don't think you would be easy to blackmail' (Richard Ellmann, *Oscar Wilde*, 1990, p. 538).

---

**GLOSSARY**

| | |
|---|---|
| 130 | *Émaux et Camées*   enamels and cameos |
| | *du supplice encore mal lavée*   still unwashed from torture |
| | *doigts de faune*   faun's fingers |
| | Sur une gamme … 'Like a chromatic scale, her collar of pearly waters, the Venus of the Adriatic lifts her pink and white body from the water. Her domes above the blue waves follow the arc of a phrase like rounded throats uttering a sigh of love. The skiff arrives and sets me down, throwing its moorings round a pillar before a pink façade on the marble of a stair.' |
| 131 | Lido   resort near Venice |
| | *monstre charmant*   in Gautier's poem, the statue of a hermaphrodite |
| 132 | Natural Science Tripos   the examination for the degree of BA |

## CHAPTER 15

- Dorian attends a party.
- During the flirtation and gossip Dorian hides his feelings, but Lord Henry insists on asking where he was the night before.
- Dorian leaves and takes a hansom cab to a destination near the river.

That evening Dorian goes to a party hosted by Lady Narborough. The guests bore him, but Lord Henry arrives in time for dinner. They gossip and flirt with their hostess, who tells Dorian that she will find him a wife. When the sexes divide after dinner, Lord Henry expresses concern for Dorian, who seems unwell.

They discuss a house party Dorian is to hold at Selby, his country home. The Duchess of Monmouth, who is 'devoted' (p. 143) to Dorian, will be attending, with her husband. Lord Henry asks Dorian where he was the previous night. Dorian is irritated, and eventually leaves.

Once home, Dorian burns Basil's things. He goes to the cabinet in his library where there is a box of opium. Then, dressed in 'common' clothes, he quietly leaves the house and hails a hansom cab. The driver is not enthusiastic about their destination.

**CONTEXT**

Marlowe's Faustus sells his soul for twenty-four years of knowledge and power, but much of what he does is rather trivial, such as playing practical jokes on the Pope.

## COMMENTARY

This chapter begins the most substantial section – four chapters – specially written for the 1891 edition. They were some of the most highly praised, with critics as different as the aesthete Walter Pater and the gossipy journalist Frank Harris united in appreciation of the social satire. Pater especially valued the tension between the comedy and Dorian's rising terror (Norton Edition, p. 135).

We watch a man who has committed the most terrible of acts being polite to 'middle-aged mediocrities' he dislikes to avoid suspicion (p. 140). This forms a sharp contrast with Dorian's entertainments in Chapter 11, when his parties led young men to see in him 'a type that was to combine something of the real culture of the scholar with all the grace and distinction and perfect manner of a citizen of the world' (p. 103).

Dorian's enjoyment of 'the terrible pleasure of a double life' (p. 139) suggests that murder has deepened his narcissism. Rather than practising true hedonism, which is about responding to the world, he is now focused on himself. The sense of possibilities wasted is intensified by an undertone of sadness that permeates this chapter. Even Lord Henry (whose insistent fuss over Dorian's health absurdly transforms the arch-cynic into a new Basil) is subdued.

The only characters with real vitality here are women. When they conform to custom and withdraw after dinner, Dorian and Lord Henry are dependent on each other for entertainment (and are rude enough to change seats in order to avoid the bores). Yet the women are subject to petty restrictions that Dorian and Lord Henry would never have to face.

Lady Narborough's energy has found some odd but respectable outlets, such as designing her husband's tomb and finding husbands for her daughters (p. 139). Witty remarks by the men about her racier counterpart, Madame de Ferrol, suggest veiled contempt: when everyone claims to be in love with a woman in this narrow world, it is an indication of her availability. Lady Narborough's most extended passage of flirtation with Lord Henry is a joke about her 'short frocks' (p. 141), a cruel reminder of the loss of her own youth. However, it is not Lady Narborough but the eternally youthful Dorian who wishes 'it were *fin du globe*' (p. 142) (the end of the world). Meanwhile, the younger woman who evidently loves him is already turning into a version of Lady Narborough, with a tedious husband who cannot match her cleverness.

Lord Henry, for all his subversive wit, and Dorian, with his boundless future, are indifferent to the rights of these intelligent and

---

**CONTEXT**

One of the company (who has a non-speaking part here) is Mrs Erlynne, 'a pushing nobody with a delightful lisp and Venetian-red hair' (p. 140). She subsequently had a major role in Wilde's 1892 play *Lady Windermere's Fan,* in which she proves to have both a scandalous past and a kind heart. Her appearance is modelled on that of Wilde's friend Lily Langtry.

 **QUESTION**

Wilde recycled the line about Madame de Ferrol's hair turning 'quite gold from grief' in Act I of *The Importance of Being Earnest.* How does the context affect the way we understand these lines?

resourceful women. They both seem to find *fin du globe* more acceptable than change and are content to leave power in the hands of mediocre men like Chapman with his 'inherited stupidity' (p. 143).

Throughout this episode the pleasures of the senses seem to be deserting Dorian. Not only does he drink champagne purely to quench his thirst, but when he turns to opium, it seems that the drug alone is not enough, and he needs a rougher setting to enhance its effects. Once again, the clock strikes: this time it is midnight, as if to suggest that time is running out for Dorian.

**GLOSSARY**

| | |
|---|---|
| 138 | mausoleum a magnificent tomb, often the size of a small room |
| 140 | *chaudfroid* meat or fish in an aspic jelly |
| 141 | *décolletée* wearing a low-necked dress |
| | *trop de zêle ... Trop d'audace* too keen ... too daring |
| 144 | feet of clay an allusion to Daniel 2, in which the king dreams of a statue with a head of gold, a body of various metals and feet of clay |
| 145 | pastilles pills of compressed incense for burning |
| | green paste opium in a form ready to be smoked |

## CHAPTER 16

- Dorian goes to the East End in search of opium.
- He meets Adrian Singleton, disgraced and disowned by his family and friends.
- A woman Dorian once knew abuses him and uses the name 'Prince Charming'.
- James Vane springs out of the shadows with a gun. When Vane speaks of the time elapsed since Sibyl's death, Dorian shows him his youthful face and Vane lets him go.
- The woman tells Vane that Dorian's face has looked the same for eighteen years.

Dorian, increasingly troubled and depressed, journeys in the cab towards the opium dens of the East End. Arriving at his chosen spot, he meets Adrian Singleton, a young man whom he has known in the past. Singleton tells him that he is now ostracised by his own circle and has been refused the money to go abroad. Wishing to shake Singleton off, Dorian says that he is going somewhere else, but invites Singleton for a drink first. Dorian is approached at the bar by an angry woman and throws down some money to get rid of her.

As Dorian bids goodbye to Adrian and leaves, the woman taunts him with the name 'Prince Charming'. Dorian hurries to his destination, reflecting on what he has done to Adrian. He is grabbed by the throat and finds himself facing James Vane, who is holding a revolver and claiming Dorian's life for Sibyl's. Vane has been hunting Dorian for years and has finally heard the name 'Prince Charming', which has identified him.

Dorian recovers enough self-assurance to ask James when his sister died. When James says that it was eighteen years ago, Dorian tells him to look at him in the light of the streetlamp. James sees what seems to be a boy of twenty. Horrified, he lets Dorian go – but the woman from the bar emerges from the shadows to tell him that 'Prince Charming' destroyed her almost eighteen years ago.

 **CHECK THE BOOK**

In 'The Man with the Twisted Lip', which first appeared in the *Strand Magazine* in 1891 and can be found in *The Adventures of Sherlock Holmes,* Holmes solves the mystery by disguising himself as an opium smoker, too listless to appear dangerous, so as to gather intelligence on 'the vilest murder trap on the whole river-side'.

**CHECK THE BOOK**

Virginia Berridge's *Opium and the People* (1999) outlines the importation, cultivation and use of opium in Britain through the nineteenth century.

## COMMENTARY

While Dorian's remark to Basil that 'each of us has Heaven and Hell in him' (p. 125) is probably the closest that the novel comes to articulating a religious conviction, the **imagery** of this chapter is saturated with biblical phrases and ideas: 'innocent blood' and 'atonement' suggest the Gospels, and crushing a snake underfoot (p. 146) is the task foretold for the fallen Eve in the Book of Genesis.

The Gothic landscape of darkness cut by flames (Limehouse, where Chinese sailors settled in large numbers, was named for the kilns that burnt lime there) suggests that Dorian is journeying into a physical hell. This hell is uncompromisingly real. Details such as the pavement slime 'like a wet mackintosh' (p. 147) are as sensuously described as Dorian's own luxurious settings, and make it clear that this is not a drug-induced vision. (Though in frantic pursuit of oblivion, Dorian never manages to get so much as a drink.)

No longer the innocent in Eden, Dorian is identified with Lucifer, the angel who fell through pride, 'that high spirit, that morning-star of evil' (p. 150). This image, derived from Milton's Satan in *Paradise Lost*, was taken up by the Romantic poets, especially Byron in his 1812 poem *Childe Harold*, to express the personification of defiant individualism. The qualities of the Byronic hero, a champion of liberty with a burden of sorrows that gave him an attractive and sinister glamour, can be seen also in figures such as *Jane Eyre*'s Mr Rochester and Sherlock Holmes.

If the Byronic Satan represents pride and rebellion, Dorian does not really manage to sustain this identity. James Vane reduces him to stammering panic and he saves himself only by deception. Dorian's dismissal of the apologetically decent Vane with 'You have been on the brink of committing a terrible crime, my man' (p. 151) is pompous and shrill, reeking of class consciousness rather than Satanic power.

One nightmarish aspect of this urban hell is its many reminders of Dorian's victims. (Similarly, Shakespeare's Richard III spends his last night on earth tormented by the ghosts of those he has killed.)

There is Adrian Singleton, whose yellow hair makes him a distorting mirror of Dorian. Recognition of this prompts Dorian's fleeting pity before he decides that 'One's days were still too brief to take the burden of another's errors' (p. 150), an inappropriate thought for a man who never grows old. There is a sudden glimpse of a man wearing an ulster, the coat favoured by Basil. Sibyl Vane is represented by a woman who might be her mirror, speaking a line Sibyl herself could utter: 'it's nigh on eighteen years since Prince Charming made me what I am' (p. 152). The woman's fear of Dorian, as well as her ruined looks, suggest the fate that might have awaited Sibyl if she had lived.

Dorian's choice of 'Prince Charming' as the pseudonym for his drug adventures is more than insensitive. It suggests that part of his pleasure lies in the contrast between his own body and the ruin of those of his companions.

## GLOSSARY

| | |
|---|---|
| 147 | **brickfields** site where clay could be found and bricks made from it |
| | **marionettes** puppets, a recurring image (pp. 132, 150) |
| 148 | **reflectors** bits of bright metal to enhance the light from a gas lamp |
| | **Malays** opium accounted for a large portion of the taxes collected in Malaya, a British colony until 1946 when it became part of Malaysia |
| 149 | **Malay crease** from *keris*, a dagger with a wavy blade |
| 150 | **morning-star of evil** Satan, also known as Lucifer, the morning star |

**CONTEXT**

When Wilde was in prison and was about to be dragged by Queensberry into the bankruptcy court, Bosie sent him a message via the solicitor's clerk: 'Prince Fleur-de-Lys wishes to be remembered to you.' Wilde reproached him in *De Profundis*: 'Nothing that had happened had made you realise a single thing. You were in your own eyes still the graceful prince of a trivial comedy' (Merlin Holland, *Complete Works of Oscar Wilde*, 1998, p. 901). Given that Bosie claimed to have read *Dorian Gray* many times, he clearly had no sense of propriety or indeed of **irony**.

## CHAPTER 17

- Dorian entertains guests at a house party, and flirts with the Duchess of Monmouth.
- While Dorian goes to pick her some orchids, Lord Henry warns the Duchess that he is dangerous.
- Dorian faints, and we learn that he has seen the face of James Vane through the window.

At the conservatory of his country home, Selby Royal, Dorian is entertaining the Duchess of Monmouth, her dull husband, Lady Narborough and Lord Henry. Lord Henry and the Duchess discuss the state of the nation. Tiring of Lord Henry's cynicism, the Duchess demands a change of subject and he tells her Dorian's old nickname, 'Prince Charming'. This troubles Dorian.

The topic shifts to that of love, and the different ways men and women experience it. Dorian goes to choose orchids for the Duchess, and Lord Henry warns her that her flirtation is a dangerous one. They are interrupted by a groan: Dorian has fainted.

Dorian refuses to spend the evening alone in his room, and dresses for dinner in a state of terror. He has seen James Vane looking in through the window.

## COMMENTARY

Much of this chapter is in dialogue, with no added details about the speakers. Anyone familiar with Wilde could identify the lines as his. However, few people could confidently say which of his works they come from, and Wilde himself even recycled some of them.

The banter is typical of his **social comedies**. The snap and speed indicate that it is a form of flirtation. It is difficult for a couple to speak aloud exchanges such as this without looking straight into each other's eyes:

**CONTEXT**

George Meredith's *An Essay on Comedy and the Uses of the Comic Spirit* (1897), a version of the highly influential lecture given by the novelist in 1877, is especially interested in witty battles between the sexes of the kind shown here and in Wilde's comedies, as well as in his own novels such as *Diana of The Crossways*. Meredith suggested that real comedy is only possible when the sexes have a degree of equality and that women should see it as a valuable weapon in defeating prejudice.

'I am on the side of the Trojans. They fought for a woman.'

'They were defeated.' (p. 156)

There are also cues for compliments at regular intervals, like the Duchess's mention of her hat. They may raise the temperature or, as here, be ignored, making a new verbal strategy necessary. However, it is the particular context of the lines that gives them a unique colouring. The underlying and unacknowledged emotions and relationships – known in the theatre as **subtext** – are often complex. Here there is an undertone of sadness and even menace.

Lord Henry's speech about words and names is a bravura display of his wit. The company stand back and enjoy it, occasionally offering a cue for him to continue. In most of Wilde's party scenes there is a resident wit of this kind, whose role in the story can be benevolent or dangerous. Lord Henry's choice of topic is **ironic**: it not only reminds us of the hypocrisy – mostly sexual – of the company as a whole but culminates with a phrase that Dorian does not want to hear. All his delight in role-playing is undermined by this reminder of his nickname 'Prince Charming' – now, with James Vane at large, a potentially lethal label to carry.

If playful rechristening carries ironic and dangerous connotations, so does the witty debate on love. The Duchess's avowal that 'you men love with your eyes' (p. 155) is, from her point of view, just a way of pointing out that beauty is only skin deep. The converse, that 'we women … love with our ears' (p. 155), is a compliment to Lord Henry's wit, possibly to make Dorian jealous. The reader knows, however, that the line is spoken to a man in thrall to his own beauty, on the brink of paying a terrible price for it.

If the scene seems to be pointing towards death for Dorian, there is also a hint that the outcome may be painful for others. When Lord Henry declares that one should experience love often, the Duchess's query, 'Even when one has been wounded by it?' (p. 156), is only thinly disguised as a joke. The pause suggests she is thinking carefully before making this remark. Is she implying that Lord Henry loves Dorian, and is not loved in return? Or is it a coded

> **CONTEXT**
>
> The French writer André Gide recalls in his memoirs that Wilde said to him, 'You listen with your eyes' (*Oscar Wilde*, 1949).

**QUESTION**

Lord Henry names 'ugliness' as one of the 'Seven Deadly Virtues'. Based on your knowledge of the text, what do you think he would nominate as the other six? Do you think Basil would agree with his choice?

statement to Dorian that she is willing to risk the consequences of an affair? Dorian's abrupt departure suggests that he has no intention of treating her with tenderness. Will the Duchess's name also be one added to the growing list of the disgraced?

## GLOSSARY

| 153 | **smoking-suits** suits designed for indoor wear |
|---|---|
| 154 | **tilt** fight with a lance on horseback, like a knight of old |
| | **seven deadly sins** Pride, Anger, Envy, Greed, Lust, Sloth and Avarice |
| 155 | **labyrinth** a maze |
| 156 | **Trojans** Paris, Prince of Troy, eloped with Helen, the wife of Menelaus of Sparta, and started a ten-year war between Greeks and Trojans |
| | *riposte* a metaphor from fencing, though here it is verbal |
| 157 | **Parthian manner** the Parthians used to fire arrows while retreating from the enemy |

## CHAPTER 18

- Terrified, Dorian remains in his room for three days, before going out to join a shooting party.
- Dorian cries out to the Duchess's brother not to shoot a hare, but the gun is fired and a man is shot by accident. The keeper tells Dorian that the man is a stranger, a sailor.
- Dorian views the body. It is that of James Vane. Dorian decides that he is now safe.

Dorian is increasingly afraid and can barely leave his room. He tells himself that he has imagined James Vane out of guilt, but the thought of being tormented all his life by such imaginings reduces him to tears.

After three days he goes out and joins a shooting party. Seeing the Duchess's brother Geoffrey about to shoot a hare, he cries out to him to let the creature live. Geoffrey shoots anyway, and kills a man. Dorian calls off the shoot, and tells Lord Henry that he fears it is a bad omen. He will not accept Lord Henry's rational reply, claiming that he can hear the wings of Death in the air (p. 161).

A note from the Duchess arrives. Dorian goes in to meet her, with Lord Henry, who makes a flippant remark about the shooting to the effect that he would 'like to know someone who had committed a real murder' (p. 162). Almost fainting with terror, Dorian retires to his room. Lord Henry asks the Duchess about her feelings for Dorian.

Dorian prepares to leave for town. The head gamekeeper arrives, and Dorian offers financial help for the family of the dead man, assuming that he is local. The keeper tells him the man was a stranger, possibly a sailor. Dorian gallops to the farm where the body is laid out. It is James Vane. As Dorian returns home he weeps, feeling that he is now safe.

## COMMENTARY

The first scene of the novel took place in summer. As the **narrative** is drawing to a close, it is icy winter. This is the first time we see Dorian in anything resembling a natural landscape, and he seems like a hunted animal gone to earth.

The chapter as a whole is scathing about the hunting fraternity: Sir Geoffrey's instant reaction to shooting a man is that he is 'spoiling my shooting for the day' (p. 160). Surprisingly, the urbane and urban Lord Henry says much the same thing. Perhaps he wants to stress that he is a true aristocrat – Dorian, after all, is only high-born on one side of the family.

In his remark that 'the whole thing is hideous and cruel' (p. 160), Dorian shares Wilde's own attitude. Act I of *A Woman of No Importance* contains the famous definition of hunting as 'the unspeakable in full pursuit of the uneatable'. However, Dorian's compassion for hunted things springs from the fact that he is one of them.

**CONTEXT**

The thundering hooves of Dorian's horse as he rides to see the corpse of James Vane add to the Gothic horror of the chapter with their suggestion of a heartbeat and are reminiscent of *The Tell-Tale Heart*, a tale of terror by Edgar Allan Poe first published in 1843. The **narrator** describes his murder of an old man. He hides the body by cutting it into pieces and hiding it under the floorboards. Ultimately his guilt manifests itself in the hallucination that the man's heart is still beating beneath the floor.

**QUESTION**

Dorian is an aristocrat on his mother's side and a 'mere nobody' (p. 28) on the other. How affected do you think Dorian is by his mixed heritage?

Some of Dorian's reflections in this chapter have a **metafictional** element as he ponders the role of the imagination. Like Miss Prism in *The Importance of Being Earnest*, he reflects that 'The good end happily, the bad unhappily: that is what fiction means', whereas in real life criminals get away with their crimes. While we would not expect Dorian to contemplate his own status as a fictional character, it seems **ironic** that he does not consider that his portrait is the stuff of legends. In most of them the bad *do* end unhappily, and the outcome of his own life may be like fiction in this respect.

Dorian invents his own comforting fiction about the fate of James Vane (even including the sinking of his ship) in a style oddly reminiscent of Sibyl's improvisations in Chapter 5. He also rejoices that 'the mask of youth had saved him' (p. 158), as if the 'mask' were an identity like 'Prince Charming' that he can choose to assume, rather than a supernatural phenomenon he cannot explain or control. But his imagination is affecting him with physical force strong enough to chill the air (p. 158). The clear division between real and fictional seems to be eroding.

Dorian identifies with Shakespeare's Macbeth. Macbeth kills: once he is a murderer, he has to go on killing in order to survive, and the ghost of one of his victims arrives at a banquet to torment him. While there are no ghosts in this novel, Dorian is haunted by his memory of the murder and for the first time since it took place (p. 158) thinks of Basil not as 'the thing' he must dispose of but as 'his friend' (p. 158).

The end of the chapter, with Dorian in a state of smug security, seems to be cheating us of the kind of fictional conclusion on which he has been brooding. A Victorian detective story invariably ended with an arrest. A **melodrama** with an honest sailor hero let the hero kill the **villain**, not get shot in a random accident. However, the final **tableau**, Dorian drawing a veil to reveal a hidden face, is an image we have seen before: Dorian drawing the curtain away from the portrait. James Vane, Dorian's opposite in every way, suddenly becomes a mirror or reminder of the absent picture that is Dorian's secret self. The story is not yet over.

## CHAPTER 19

- Dorian dines with Lord Henry, and announces that he has changed.
- He thinks his first 'good action' was not to seduce a young village girl. Lord Henry is not so sure.
- They talk about Basil and the painting.
- Lord Henry raises the subject of the soul.
- Dorian leaves. He accuses Lord Henry of 'poisoning' him with a book.

 **QUESTION**

In the *Lippincott's* version, this chapter follows immediately after the death of Basil. What effect do you think the intervening chapters have on our view of the **narrative**? Which version do you prefer?

Dorian is dining with Lord Henry, and tells him that he is going to be good. He describes his first 'good action' (p. 167): while staying in the country he had formed an attachment to a young village girl, Hetty, and had asked her to go away with him, but he 'spared' her by leaving. Lord Henry points out that he has probably made her unhappy with her situation in life.

The conversation shifts to the disappearance of Basil. Lord Henry is not interested, and persuades Dorian to play the piano for him. Dorian asks, 'What would you say, Harry, if I told you that I had murdered Basil?' (p. 168). Lord Henry tells him he is incapable of crime, which is for 'the lower orders' (p. 168), and that Basil is too dull for such an interesting fate.

Lord Henry idly quotes a line he has heard from a street preacher: 'what does it profit a man if he gain the whole world and lose ... his own soul?' (p. 170). Lord Henry is disinclined to believe that the soul exists. Dorian replies that it is 'a terrible reality' (p. 170). Complaining of his age, Lord Henry praises Dorian as 'a perfect type' (p. 171) who has made his life a work of art. Dorian decides to leave, repeating his intention to be good. As Lord Henry promises that their friendship will never change, Dorian reproaches him for 'poisoning' him with a book (p. 172). Lord Henry refuses to accept this, and insists on seeing Dorian the next day.

## COMMENTARY

In this chapter Lord Henry speaks of the power of memory and how a scent, or a snatch of music, can evoke the past. The text itself makes use of this device: the action is shot through with echoes of earlier events, repeated in a darker vein.

It is May. With the image of Dorian and Lord Henry among blossoms and strawberries, the story comes full circle to the summer of Chapter 1. Dorian seems transformed since the winter, and it is as if the murder and the escape from death have resulted in another rebirth. Just as his wish gave him eighteen more years – a second youth – so the deaths of Basil and James seem to have given him new life.

Dorian plays the piano and listens to Lord Henry lecturing on life as he did all those years ago. There are differences, however. In the original version of the story, this chapter followed directly on from the one in which Alan Campbell destroys Basil's corpse. The talk about Basil here plants his memory firmly and underlines Lord Henry's refusal to consider that he could bear any responsibility for influencing Dorian. Not only is Lord Henry unable to imagine Dorian, or any of his own class, capable of killing, but his flippancy prevents what might have been Dorian's first attempt to take responsibility for his actions and admit to the murder.

**CONTEXT**

The first image in the chapter is of Henry using a finger bowl, a routine procedure at an aristocratic dinner party. But following on from so much talk of death and murder in the last few chapters, it suggests Pontius Pilate in the Gospels washing his hands as a way of refusing to take responsibility for the crucifixion of Jesus. Henry is symbolically answering in advance Dorian's accusation of 'poisoning' him with a book.

Lord Henry's final aphorism, 'Art has no influence on action' (p. 172), shows that in the course of his experiment he has learned nothing about Dorian or what makes him tick.

There is a decided shift in power relations here. Lord Henry no longer speaks in hypnotic rhythms that plunge Dorian into confusion. Instead, his speeches jump from topic to topic – Dorian, youth, boring old people, Chopin – so that he sounds almost as disorganised as his former wife, from whom he is now divorced. (Comically, he does manage to hypnotise the parrot.) Lord Henry's carefully structured **ironies** are replaced by unintentional ones, which reveal more of himself than he might wish.

For example, Lord Henry pays Dorian a classical compliment intended as a tribute to his looks and musical ability: 'It seems that you are the young Apollo, and that I am Marsyas listening to you' (p. 171). However, Marsyas, a minor river god, was punished for competing musically with Apollo by being flayed alive, and the image suggests Lord Henry's subconscious awareness of his own vulnerability. Devoid of his youth and looks, his linguistic fluency decreasing as Dorian's has grown, what does he have to offer Dorian? Lord Henry is certainly less skilful now in enticing Dorian to an engagement. After their first encounter Dorian broke several promises to be with Lord Henry, but now he gives in with a weary 'Must I really come, Harry?' (p. 173).

However, Lord Henry is refreshingly astute on the matter of Hetty Merton. Dorian's comparison of her to Perdita associates her with the Shakespearean actress Sibyl. However, in *The Winter's Tale* Perdita the shepherdess and her Prince Florizel are assertive in the face of kingly disapproval and faithful to each another. Dorian's assumption of the Florizel role while proclaiming that Hetty 'was not one of our own class, of course' (p. 166) shows that he is still recycling his 'Prince Charming' role without any sense of irony.

**CHECK THE POEM**

Browning's poem 'Bishop Blougram's Apology' describes the disturbing power of art and nature to reawaken old emotions: 'Just when we're safest, there's a sunset touch, / A fancy from a flower-bell, some one's death, / A chorus ending from Euripides, / And that's enough for fifty hopes and fears …' (lines 183–6).

**CHECK THE FILM**

In Stephen Norrington's 2003 film *The League of Extraordinary Gentlemen*, Dorian Gray is the villain, defeated by Mina Harker from *Dracula*, now a widow and a vampire. This seems a fitting end for Dorian, whose youth increasingly seems to suck the life from others as the novel progresses.

## GLOSSARY

| 167 | **copper bowl** here, a finger-bowl, used to wash the hands between courses at a formal dinner |
|-----|---|
| | **Ophelia** in *Hamlet*, Ophelia goes mad and is drowned draped in garlands of flowers and leaves |
| | **next world** Heaven or Hell – Henry does not say which |
| 168 | **vinaigrette box** smelling salts, to revive the tired or faint |
| | **Waterbury watch** cheap watch, made in Waterbury, Connecticut |
| | **Velasquez** (1599–1660) Spanish painter who strongly influenced the Impressionists |
| 170 | **his own soul** quoted from Mark 8:36 |
| | **nocturne** dreamy piece of music |
| 171 | **high stocks** high stiff band around the neck |
| | *lilas blanc* white lilac |

**QUESTION**

Lord Henry's reference to white lilac (p. 171) echoes Dorian 'burying his face in the great cool lilac blossoms' in Chapter 2 (p. 20). What effect does this echo have?

## CHAPTER 20

- Dorian walks home in a state of turmoil.
- Arriving home, he blames his youth and beauty for his corruption, and destroys his mirror.
- Dorian looks for a sign of his 'good action' in the portrait, but finds only hypocrisy.
- Hating the picture as a reproach to his conscience and evidence of the murder, he stabs it.
- Dorian is found dead, old and ugly, in front of the picture which now looks as it did when Basil painted it.

As Dorian walks home he is filled with regrets. Hating his own youth and beauty, he smashes his mirror. He comforts himself that Basil's body is gone, that James Vane is dead and that Alan has killed himself. He blames Basil for creating the picture and refuses to accept any responsibility for Alan's death.

Congratulating himself on 'sparing' Hetty, Dorian goes to look at the picture. It is even uglier, with a look of hypocrisy and bloodstains that were not there before. He wonders whether this is a sign that he should confess. Confused, he resents the picture's lack of improvement before admitting to himself that he 'spared' Hetty only as a new sensation. Concluding that the picture is the only 'evidence' of his guilt and a nagging 'conscience' that spoils his pleasure in life, he decides to destroy it and stabs it with the knife he used to kill Basil.

Hearing a cry, the servants wake up. Two passers-by fetch a policeman; he tells them that it is Dorian's house and they leave with a sneer, while the policeman watches but makes no attempt to enter. Eventually, the servants break into the room via the balcony. They find a portrait of the beautiful young Dorian. A hideous old man with a knife in his heart lies dead on the floor.

## COMMENTARY

Chapters 19 and 20 were originally a single unit, split for the 1891 edition of the text. This break at the point when Dorian is alone makes a clear signal to the reader, just as in Marlowe's *Faustus* the stage is cleared of superfluous characters for the final confrontation. This is the end of the devil's bargain, the point when the devil comes to claim his own.

Rather than facing a devil, Dorian enters a hall of mirrors. Passers-by recognise different aspects of his identity. The young men see him as a celebrity. The 'two gentlemen' (p. 177) – one of them related to one of Dorian's victims – sneer, aware of the damage he has done to others. The policeman does not try to enter the house, despite hearing the cry, as if he already recognises the house as notorious for violence but knows he cannot stop it.

Dorian himself looks into a mirror, Lord Henry's gift and the symbol of his influence. Carved with little love-gods, it is designed to make Dorian fall in love with himself. Dorian remembers a letter from a lover, whose words describe the beauty the mirror shows: 'The curves of your lips rewrite history' (p. 175). The extravagant

**CHECK THE BOOK**

Treatments of the devil's bargain show the time when the soul is finally forfeit as one that has to be faced alone. A version Wilde knew well is the ending of *Melmoth the Wanderer* (1820) by his maternal uncle, Charles Maturin (republished by World's Classics, 1989). On his final night the apparently ageless Wanderer tells his companions: 'Whatever noises you hear in the course of the awful night that is approaching, come not near this apartment, in peril of your lives … remember your lives will be the forfeit of your desperate curiosity ' (p. 540). Terrible sounds are heard from behind the door, and all that remains of the Wanderer in the morning is a handkerchief that he had been wearing round his neck.

**CONTEXT**

In the cartoon series *Family Guy*, the sister, Meg, asks the family how she looks. Stewie, the haughty baby, mutters, 'I'll put it this way: in an attic somewhere there's a portrait of you getting prettier.'

phrase is darkly **ironic**. Dorian can smash the mirror, but he cannot 'rewrite' what has been inscribed on his painted face.

The picture confirms this, faithfully updating the image of Dorian's soul: not only the 'curved wrinkle of the hypocrite' (p. 176) but blood 'even on the hand that had not held the knife' (p. 176). Dorian has committed no more actual murders, but he has denied his responsibility for the deaths of Basil, of James Vane and of Alan Campbell, only moments before. He is aware of a duty to confess to murder, but he refuses to own this thought. He prefers to attribute it to the portrait – which, of course, makes it easy for him to argue himself out of doing anything.

Dorian sees the picture, the final mirror of himself, as simultaneously the 'conscience' that tells him to confess and the one piece of evidence that links him to the crime. It is both the authentic record of his soul and a 'thing', like the corpse of Basil, which he can destroy because he feels nothing for it but revulsion.

Kenneth Womack's essay on the ethics of the soul in *Dorian Gray* offers a useful word to describe Dorian's state of mind here: 'anti-epiphany'. While an **epiphany** is a moment of life-changing revelation, the reverse is a lethal lack of clarity. Dorian has lost the ability to distinguish right from wrong and soul from body. His selfhood has broken down into nothing but corruption, disintegrating to the point where the servants, who feed, dress and care for him, cannot confirm the identity of his body. Only his rings, the symbols of his rank and wealth, remain to confirm who he was.

**GLOSSARY**

| 174 | **unsullied** pure |
| | **polished shield** an allusion to the shield of Perseus; by using his shield as a mirror in which to see her reflection, Perseus was able to cut off the head of the Medusa, who turned to stone anyone who looked at her |
| 175 | **livery** uniform |
| | **waning** growing less |
| 176 | **below-stairs** that is, in the servants' part of the house |

# EXTENDED COMMENTARIES

## TEXT 1 – CHAPTER 4: PP. 47–8

From 'As he left the room …' to '… sculpture or painting.'

Dorian has just told Lord Henry about his love for Sibyl Vane and has invited him to come to the theatre to watch her. Before they part, they arrange to include Basil in the invitation. Dorian asks Lord Henry to write to Basil, saying that he does not want to see Basil on his own as he tends to offer advice.

This is the first time in the novel that we encounter a character alone with his thoughts. Given the title, we might be surprised that it is not Dorian, especially as we have already heard Lord Henry expound his ideas at length. This passage, then, is going to reveal something new – perhaps something that contradicts what we think we already know of Lord Henry. In a work like the Shakespearean plays performed by Sibyl, this might be a moment at which Lord Henry would utter a **soliloquy**, explaining to the audience his motives for acting as he does. Here, the text is more **ambiguous**: are these Lord Henry's thoughts, or a narrator's comment, or something between the two? The passage begins with the drooping of Lord Henry's eyelids, as if he is in a trance or dream, and perhaps off guard.

Lord Henry's first 'thought' (or the **narrator**'s first comment) is that he feels no jealousy of Sibyl. This may prompt the question, 'If that is the case, why bother to mention it at all?' Jealousy is evidently on his mind. Lord Henry is keeping up his power struggle with Basil: he has gained more of Dorian's time than Basil, and has just joined Dorian in criticising their friend. Perhaps it is easier for him to deal with Dorian's 'mad adoration' (p. 47) for a vulnerable young woman than to compete with a mature artist.

There is a mild voyeurism in Lord Henry's fantasy of Dorian and the 'white girl' (p. 47) that does not fit his self-image as a detached and scientific observer, and it leads us to question whether he really is such an observer at all. His dismissal of 'natural science' – that is, chemistry, physics, biology and astronomy – as 'trivial and of no

**CHECK THE NET**

*Reading Wilde, Querying Spaces* is a website to commemorate the centenary of Wilde's imprisonment and contains a wealth of visual material from a variety of nineteenth-century publications. Go to **www.nyu.edu** and search for Oscar Wilde.

**CONTEXT**

Wilde knew what an emotive term 'vivisection' would be. In 1885 Ruskin resigned from the Slade Professorship because of Oxford's support for vivisection: 'I cannot lecture in the next room to a shrieking cat, nor address myself to the men who have been – there's no word for it' (Francis O'Gorman, *Ruskin*, 1999, p. 16).

**CONTEXT**

In Mary Shelley's *Frankenstein*, the creature reproaches his creator as Dorian blames Basil and Lord Henry: 'I will revenge my injuries. If I cannot inspire love, I will cause fear, and chiefly towards you, my arch-enemy, because my creator, do I swear inextinguishable hatred. Have a care, I will work at your destruction … I will desolate your heart.'

import' (p. 47) seems arrogant, to say the least. The use of the word 'vivisect', literally 'to cut up alive', is disturbing. What would a man who 'vivisected himself' be like? In Lord Henry's mind Dorian seems to be shifting from 'study' to guinea pig.

Lord Henry's extended **metaphor** of 'life in its curious crucible of pain and pleasure' (p. 47) invites some questions. A crucible implies that certain things have been deliberately brought together: if so, by whom? Given that Lord Henry does not seem to believe in God, it seems that he, the self-styled scientist, is the one to do the mixing. He expects to suffer in the process – but again, his metaphor is revealing. 'Sulphurous fumes' extend his previous chemical analogy, but they are also associated with the devil, and the 'misshapen dreams' (p. 47) they cause link them to opium. The effects of corrosive chemicals and opium will become important in the story in painfully literal ways, playing their part in the destruction of both Basil and Dorian.

Lord Henry goes on to consider the 'hard logic of passion' and the 'emotional coloured life of the intellect' (p. 47) as if they too were chemicals in a flask. The way he congratulates himself that Dorian's desire for Sibyl (whom he has never seen) has been created by his own words suggests that he intends this relationship to achieve 'unison' and 'discord' as he chooses. Dorian is no longer even a guinea pig: he is now Lord Henry's 'own creation' (p. 48). Surrounded by the prevalent **imagery** of corrosive chemicals and drugs, the idea carries connotations of Gothic horror: this is not a story about mentoring or personal growth, but a version of *Frankenstein*.

There is a warning note in the repeated word 'premature' (p. 48). People do not usually congratulate themselves that their child has been born before its time, as it means that it will be faced with difficulties that it is too weak to negotiate. Lord Henry envisages Dorian as one of 'life's masterpieces' (p. 48). Victor Frankenstein made a human creature, fully intending it to improve on nature; he took no kind of parental responsibility for it and it grew to hate and reproach him. Dorian's future looks less than promising.

## TEXT 2 – CHAPTER 11: PP. 111–12

From 'He had a special passion…' to 'should have been his own.'

Dorian has rejected Sibyl and learned of her suicide. His painting has begun to change and Lord Henry has sent him the book that influences his whole life. The pictures grows uglier and uglier as Dorian plunges into debauchery. In a more public way, he has plunged into the study of religion and science and is collecting jewels and embroideries.

While the effect of the whole chapter is cumulative, each detailed section has been included for its specific effect. While overall we observe Dorian's conspicuous consumption, the images that pass in front of us carry their individual weight of connotation. This section, about church vestments, is significantly separated from an earlier section where Dorian's attraction for the ritual is described (p. 106). While that section was full of movement – priests raising the holy bread, boys flinging incense, Dorian himself kneeling – here the robes are 'stored away' in 'long cedar chests' (p. 111) suggesting coffins, as if Dorian has chosen to bury the idea of religious faith.

The text raises a powerful image of disguise and concealment. The vestments, although worn by men, are the robes of the Bride of Christ, the Church, 'who must wear purple and jewels and fine linen that she may hide the pallid macerated body that is worn by the suffering that she seeks for, and wounded by self-inflicted pain' (p. 111). The Church, in other words, conceals the pain of self-sacrifice, martyrdom and penance beneath a beautiful robe – the converse of Dorian's beauty that cloaks only wickedness.

The inventory of this part of his collection begins with two copes – a kind of cloak that is worn in processions and solemn ceremonies other than the Mass. The first one described is red, the colour in which martyrs are celebrated, picking up on the idea of suffering concealed in beauty. The second, in green, carries an image of Saint Sebastian, shot to death with arrows for his faith – a saint who is often portrayed more or less nude. Sebastian was beloved of the Roman emperor who killed him, and is thus linked to Antinoüs,

 **CHECK THE NET**

To see something like the beautiful copes described here, go to **www. vam.ac.uk** and type 'Syon cope' into the search box.

**CONTEXT**

In the Greek Orthodox church, the priest recites a special prayer while putting on his robes that compares his garments to the wedding dress of the Bride of Christ.

**CONTEXT**

During his student travels with Mahaffy, Wilde was deeply impressed by Guido Reni's painting of Saint Sebastian in Genoa. He took the name 'Sebastian Melmoth' when living in exile.

with whom Dorian is compared more than once (for example, in Basil's reference to 'Adrian's barge', p. 92).

After these processional garments, the text moves on to a description of the robes for the most sacred of all rites, the Mass. We are, perhaps, following Dorian's own imaginative journey as he considers his collection. The chasuble, a sleeveless outer garment rather like a poncho, is used when the priest celebrates the sacrament and symbolises the yoke of Christ, the taking on of a burden. This is something that Dorian does not do, making no more commitment to Catholicism than to his other masks. Blue is a colour associated with the Virgin Mary; gold is associated with Easter. Dorian has chosen garments that celebrate birth at Christmas and eternal life at the Resurrection.

Dorian seems to be collecting robes to symbolise every stage of his endless existence. He even owns some items used during the Mass: 'dalmatics', the simple garments which go under the more showy chasuble, and even 'sudaria', napkins used to dry perspiration from the priest's forehead. This suggests an actor obsessively gathering every prop or costume that might help him with his role. Is Dorian, perhaps, identifying more closely than he realises with the **narrative** of suffering and redemption that is performed in the Mass? He even covers the picture with a 'pall' (p. 112), a cloth used to drape a coffin, as if somehow it too can be incorporated in his imaginative escape to a dream of religion.

## TEXT 3 – CHAPTER 14: PP. 133–7

From 'Campbell took a chair …' to '… Campbell made no answer.'

Dorian has killed Basil. He has now summoned Alan Campbell, to whom he was once close, to help him dispose of the body. We have been given a great deal of unspecific information about Dorian's life. The text speaks of rumours, which it substantiates with details not of his actions but of the results: the reported shame and misery of other people and the changes in the portrait. This time it is different. Not only is one of the victims allowed a voice of his own, but we actually see Dorian plan and execute the crime of blackmail.

In a society where reputation – sexual and financial – was paramount, any of Wilde's readers, even those not in fear of the Criminal Law Amendment Act, could understand this as an indication of how evil Dorian has become. Blackmail is a crime that feeds like a vampire on the pain of others. The absence of detail makes this episode resemble a kind of manual for would-be blackmailers. Nobody spells out what Alan has done or what will happen if he does not co-operate, and even if Victorian censorship permitted this it would be unnecessary. The rules of blackmail are always the same: to be successful it must be ruthless.

The most chilling aspect of the episode is that from the first demand to the final surrender it is framed by Dorian's 'pity' (p. 133). He can afford this emotion precisely because he intends to ignore it. The moment Alan sits down to listen, he has ensured that he will not leave until the transaction is over.

A blackmailer exploiting a past relationship may try to move his victim emotionally. Dorian shows an assured technique here, making fleeting **allusions** to his own pain: 'You don't know what he had made me suffer' (p. 134); 'I almost fainted with terror', 'They will hang me' (p. 135). However, he does not dwell on it, merely giving Alan a chance to reflect on any feelings he may still have for Dorian. The emotion needs to be balanced by the tacit assurance that the blackmailer is capable of doing whatever is necessary. Dorian is willing to grovel, to use words like 'beg' and 'entreat' (p. 135). But he also lets Alan know that he is capable of murder. His admission – following on from his remark that the situation is 'a matter of life and death … and to more than one person' (p. 133) – could be read as a threat as well as a confession. It is clearly desirable to make the victim feel that surrender is inevitable.

Alan is wrong to say that Lord Henry has taught Dorian nothing about psychology: Dorian has learned from Lord Henry the technique of hypnotic speech. He plies Alan with false logic. Alan is a scientist, and scientists handle dead bodies; therefore this would be no different from an experiment. Dorian also hints that Alan's treatment of dead bodies makes him as callous as Dorian is

> **CONTEXT**
>
> Ibsen's 1879 play *A Doll's House,* staged in England in 1889 when it caused tremendous controversy, showed a woman being blackmailed by a money lender after she had forged her husband's name to guarantee the loan. She is so terrified by the prospect of disgrace that she sees herself as an unfit mother to her children and contemplates suicide.

himself. This prepares the ground for a final master-stroke. The victim is convinced that the whole situation is his fault. Dorian's accusation 'You treated me as no man has ever dared to treat me' (p. 136) has such conviction that we may wonder whether he really believes this to be the case himself. The frightening addition 'no living man at least' (p. 136) suggests that he now thinks of blackmail as a relatively lenient punishment for a man who has crossed him.

## TEXT 4 – CHAPTER 18: PP. 162–3

From 'Ah! Here is the Duchess …' to '… scarlet fruit.'

At Dorian's shooting party, the Duchess's brother has accidentally killed James Vane after Dorian has tried to stop him shooting a hare. Dorian is deeply disturbed and irritated by a blatant attempt by the Duchess to get him alone. This episode shows different kinds of concealment: the coded sexual intrigues of the aristocracy mingle with Dorian's public face concealing blind terror.

Dorian and Lord Henry are talking with unusual intimacy and even affection as the Duchess appears. Dorian has to stage surprise and pleasure at seeing her, even though he is in no mood to flirt. She is keen for details of the accident, possibly because showing sympathy will help her to get close to Dorian. Dorian deftly avoids this with a further show of 'good manners': convention dictated that one should not upset ladies with unpleasant information.

Lord Henry unwittingly destroys Dorian's peace completely with 'I should like to know someone who had committed a real murder' (p. 162). Dorian's near-faint suggests that he reads this as a veiled accusation. His presence of mind here is remarkable, revealing his growing talent for deceit. He promptly breaks any apparent link between Lord Henry's remark and his own guilt by pretending that the faint preceded it and even stopped him hearing it. He then exploits his evident illness to escape both Lord Henry's curiosity and the Duchess's sexual demands.

**CONTEXT**

In Shakespeare's play, Hamlet stages a murder play that he hopes will make his uncle reveal by his reaction that he has murdered Hamlet's father. Dorian may suspect that Lord Henry's flippant remark has been made for the same reason.

The 'glass door' (p. 162) that closes behind him is a vivid symbol of Dorian's life. He must keep his distance even though, as an object of desire, he is constantly looked at. But it also adds to the sense that Dorian is not the only one for whom doors are closing. This whole class is in decay. Lord Henry breaks the carefully sustained surface to ask a very direct question. Said aloud, it could have a number of inflections: is he simply inquiring about the Duchess's feelings, or does he say 'Are *you* very much in love with him?' (p. 162), implying that they are both in the same boat? The two agree that 'one may lose one's way', and while they are speaking about love the 'mist' of uncertainty pervades the whole landscape (p. 162). The old order, as well as love, is ending in disillusion.

Implicitly they acknowledge that they are unwilling to change the status quo. Lord Henry takes for granted that the Duchess would 'miss' the 'strawberry leaves' (p. 163) – the title she would lose if her affairs led to divorce. As the second son, he no doubt 'misses' the title he has never had. The Duchess agrees she 'will not part with a petal' (p. 163), even though the marriage is wretched. They are trapped in their stale world, and they know it.

> **CONTEXT**
>
> Throughout the 1880s there were calls for the abolition of the House of Lords. Lord Curzon, like the Duchess a militant Tory, announced that 'All civilization has been the work of aristocracies'.

## PART THREE

## CRITICAL APPROACHES

# CHARACTERISATION

The earlier Victorians were preoccupied with the idea of 'character', the unique, unchanging essence of the person. To 'possess character' was to have integrity. However, with science continually revealing how much humans shared with the rest of the animal world, it became harder to hold on to this idea of a single, unchanging human essence as opposed to the idea of a nature formed by a constant process of adaptation to environment, circumstances and will. As the century wore on, the word 'personality' came into common use. The word derives from the Latin *persona,* meaning an actor's mask. Psychologists and literary practitioners alike were interested in the idea that someone could have more than one personality, and that these might be in conflict or even concealed from one another.

All the characters in the novel, consciously or unconsciously, assume more than one role or identity. For some, like Sibyl and her mother, it is a profession, but each has a different relationship to the roles that he or she plays. For the aristocrats, the mask of manners is a device to preserve the ordered surface of superiority from which their social group derives much of its power. Individuals use it to conceal private desires from some people while expressing them to others. But there is also a collective mask hiding ugly realities. Dorian's 'mask' of an innocent face is a symbol of the ability of his class to get away with murder. Society ensures that Lord Kelso's crime is hidden from the world. He is punished for murder only by temporary social exclusion: he ate 'his chop alone at the club for some time afterwards' (p. 29).

Dorian wants to become 'a being with myriad lives and myriad sensations' (p. 113), entering imaginatively into other lives, and adopting a variety of costumes, disguises and mind-altering drugs, but this is also true of most of the characters. The continual interplay of masks and identities makes it difficult to state of anyone in the novel (as one can with, say, a character in Jane Austen) 'this is what this person is like'. We need to look at how each mask is used,

**QUESTION**

Among the items that appeared in *Lippincott's Magazine* alongside the original *Dorian Gray* were an article on palmistry, a serial thriller and a feature called 'The Indissolubility of Marriage'. If you were including the novel in a collection today, what fiction or non-fiction would you choose to go with it?

how each role is played, how the performance affects others and what possibilities are opened or closed for the player. You may find it hard to reach a conclusion about the characters, or that you judge them quite differently from other readers. This is one of the reasons *Dorian Gray* continues to be read and re-read.

## BASIL HALLWARD

Nobody actually uses the phrase 'Good old Basil', but they constantly seem about to. Dorian tells him that 'if I were in trouble … I would sooner go to you' (p. 94), although he never really realises that he *is* in trouble until Basil is dead. This fits his friend's self-effacing nature: only in Basil's absence can his moral strictures begin to be heard. At the close of the novel Lord Henry dismisses Basil as a 'bore' and his work as 'that curious mixture of bad painting and good intentions that always entitles a man to be called a representative British artist' (p. 169). 'Bore' is a cruel description, but if Basil's art does decline it is a measure of the sacrifices he has made.

Basil is the only central character with a sense of right and wrong. For a long time he refuses to believe that his friends can commit an evil action, and while he cheerfully warns Dorian about Lord Henry's bad influence, he also assumes that Lord Henry's cynicism is 'simply a pose' (p. 7). When he can no longer ignore the rumours about Dorian, he willingly turns himself into an 'amateur curate' (p. 120) and struggles with a vocabulary of sin and redemption not altogether natural to him. If this makes him a 'bore' it is because he has consciously taken the role of Good Angel, never as exciting as that of tempter.

Most of the roles Basil chooses diminish rather than enhance his ego. He enters the houses of the upper classes as a necessary evil – 'With an evening coat, and a white tie … anybody, even a stockbroker, can gain a reputation for being civilised' (pp. 8–9) – but has no illusions about their world. 'English society is all wrong' (p. 120), he tells Dorian, but he will not accept this as an excuse for personal immorality. Although his studio, where he receives other people, is exotically furnished, he does not dress to advertise his status. Dorian teases him for his modest luggage – 'What a way for a

> **CONTEXT**
>
> The story of Pygmalion, the sculptor who falls in love with the statue he has created that is then brought to life by the goddess Aphrodite, was the subject of a series of paintings by the Pre-Raphaelite artist Edward Burne-Jones in 1878. Entitled *The Heart Desires, The Hand Refrains, The Godhead Fires* and *The Soul Attains,* they show the progress of the statue from conception, through divine awakening, to life as a real woman.

fashionable painter to travel!' (p. 118) – and Lord Henry mocks his cheap watch. He effaces himself even to his servants: 'When I leave town now I never tell my people where I am going' (p. 7).

This desire *not* to be a 'personality' contrasts with the attitudes of Dorian and Lord Henry and is consistent with Basil's love for Dorian, perpetually unrequited and always proof against all the petty rejections he receives as Dorian is increasingly drawn to Lord Henry. There are two sides to this silent adoration. One is negative in its effects. Basil finds Lord Henry's description of his aunt who 'treats her guests exactly as an auctioneer treats his goods' (p. 10) unkind, but it does not occur to him that his praise of Dorian, which exhausts language itself ('The merely visible presence of this lad – for he seems to me little more than a lad, though he is really over twenty – his merely visible presence – ah!', p. 12), turns him into an object of desire for the predatory Lord Henry, who sets to work on Dorian immediately.

Basil is the reverse of Lord Henry's ideal of 'one man to live his life out fully and completely … to give form to every feeling, expression to every thought, reality to every dream' (p. 18). Like Dr Jekyll, he denies himself to a dangerous degree (see **Literary background: The Victorian Gothic**). He does not tell Dorian of his feelings until the picture has already begun to change. His original determination that Dorian 'shall never know'(p. 12) may spring from fear of rejection or a conviction that homosexual desire is forbidden, but this refusal to articulate his longing means that it remains at the level of 'worship' – a word Basil uses frequently – rather than ordinary love, which must come to terms with the flaws of the beloved.

Basil's self-denial, however, also makes him the heart of the story. He would rather destroy the picture than let it provoke a quarrel between Lord Henry and Dorian. He crushes his own jealousy to voice approval of the love between Dorian and Sibyl, abandoning class prejudice as well as his own hopes. This does more than reveal his generosity of spirit. It also implicitly poses a question which Lord Henry never asks while preaching self-fulfilment: where do the desires of others fit in? For most people it is impossible to give way to *every* desire without involving someone else.

**CHECK THE BOOK**

You can see Burne-Jones's cartoon of an artist trying to climb inside his own painting in R. K. R Thornton's study *The Decadent Dilemma* (1983).

Once Basil has confessed his love, he graciously accepts that no means no and settles for the role of trusted friend. However, if we believe Lord Henry's judgement that Basil's later work is inferior to the portrait, he does so at a cost. As an unrequited lover, as the artist searching to express 'the wonder' (p. 12) of life, and as the friend who reminds others of those better selves they could be, Basil is the embodiment of longing, while Lord Henry and Dorian end with their desires burnt out. Basil may be a bore to them – and even, in his role of dull but worthy Good Angel, to the reader – but we are also aware that his painful inner life is anything but tedious.

## LORD HENRY

Lord Henry is an aristocrat. His place in the family is a cause of resentment – 'my elder brother won't die, and my younger brothers never seem to do anything else' (p. 10) – but it also means that he has rank without responsibility. While scathing about the faults of his class, he seems to have little personal experience of life outside it; certainly we only see him within the setting of polite society. He can be politically astute – as with his diagnosis of the problems of the East End: 'It is the problem of slavery, and we try to solve it by amusing the slaves' (p. 34) – but it is quite clear that he is content with the status quo.

Lord Henry's dealings with the less privileged suggest that he regards them as disposable. The death of a beater at a shoot 'does not do … It makes people think that one is a wild shot' (p. 160), and his announcement that women 'love being dominated' (p. 83) suggest that he is impervious to the changes taking place in the world. His response to a new acquaintance is to find out exactly how they fit into his tight circle. He enjoys the romance of Dorian's history, but he is also as concerned with the young man's property, inheritance and status as the last of the Kelso line as any society hostess hoping to marry off her daughters.

Lord Henry entices Dorian away from charitable work, but while his contempt for private philanthropy echoes Wilde's, its political basis is different. Wilde believed socialism should eradicate poverty. Lord Henry's belief that 'the nineteenth century has gone bankrupt through an over-expenditure of sympathy' (p. 35) is a form of social

**CHECK THE BOOK**

Lord Henry's manipulative coldness, while he remains free of any actual crime, is reminiscent of an American novel Wilde greatly admired, Nathaniel Hawthorne's *The Scarlet Letter* (1850). The heroine bears an illegitimate child in a harsh New England Puritan community. Although she eventually attains the respect of those around her, she is haunted by her elderly husband who is determined to bring down the child's clergyman father and becomes 'dark, disturbed and evil' in the process (*The Scarlet Letter*, Chapter 23).

Darwinism (see **Historical background: New sciences**) which avers that the weak should be allowed to die out. However, his sneer to the Duchess about 'the survival of the pushing' (p. 154) sounds as if he does not like the idea that the middle class should push out his own.

He sees Dorian as a scientific experiment – not his first, and with ominous precedents: 'He had begun by vivisecting himself, as he had ended by vivisecting others' (p. 47). While there is little information about Lord Henry's past, apart from the marriage he regrets, it seems clear that the degree of violence to the self implied in that word 'vivisection' has left him almost emotionless.

Dorian's attraction for Lord Henry lies in the notion that 'There was nothing that one could not do with him' (p. 31). While Lord Henry's praises of Dorian's beauty suggest erotic longing, his desire is rooted not in sex but in power. Basil may long for physical union with Dorian, but Lord Henry intends to dominate him until he has penetrated his mind and his own ideas return to him on Dorian's lips. To achieve this he relies on the power of words – at first his own to implant a desire in Dorian by hypnotising him into believing that it is already there: 'You have had passions that have made you afraid, thoughts that have filled you with terror' (p. 18). But he is also content to use the words of others and allow the 'mere cadence of the sentences, the subtle monotony of their music' in the book he has given Dorian (p. 101) to work their 'poison'.

Lord Henry's verbal fluency is a means to an end, not a source of pride. This makes him dangerous. He is not an artist, subordinating himself to the work, as Basil is. Basil is right to question whether Lord Henry means what he says. However, while Basil insists that Lord Henry is *better* than he says, Lord Henry is a hypocrite, pronouncing 'all' influence bad while making Dorian his personal project. He makes his protégé into a mirror of himself, without caring that it will inevitably be a distorting one. For example, Lord Henry's sentiments about 'the wonder of the spectacle' (p. 84) of Sibyl Vane's suicide are callous, but they are a comment on the death of a stranger. However, when Dorian calls it 'one of the great romantic tragedies of the age' (p. 88), his lack of emotional concern is truly shocking. Dorian's feelings when rejecting Sibyl were not creditable, but they were his own. As he assumes Lord Henry's mask of detachment, Lord Henry's power becomes apparent.

While Lord Henry smugly reflects on the 'perfect type' (p. 171) he has made of Dorian, it seems that he does not know what a monster he has created. More than once he tells Dorian that he is incapable of crime. He seems to have no knowledge of Dorian's life in the opium dens. He never mentions his sister's disgrace, but continues to introduce Dorian to potential lovers of his own class, out of ignorance or indifference. However, although Lord Henry plays Evil Angel to Dorian's Faust, he is mortal. As he appears at the end, 'wrinkled, and worn, and yellow' (p. 172), there is a new neediness. (He even admits to missing his wife.) Attempting to persuade Dorian to stay, he can only offer the usual, tired pleasures – music, introductions and the Club. Although he still admits to no personal longing for Dorian, and may lack the self-awareness to acknowledge it, he uses the word 'worship' here for the first time.

## DORIAN GRAY

Just after Dorian has made his fatal wish, Basil tells him 'as soon as you are dry, you shall be varnished, and framed, and sent home. Then you can do what you like with yourself' (p. 25). This joke contains a painful truth. Dorian *does* do what he likes, which is to assume a dizzying range of masks and identities, from transvestite Roman emperor to pianist, Catholic convert to blackmailer. He has many different relationships and is a patron and practitioner of the arts, retaining his ability to enchant with a Chopin nocturne even in the throes of self-examination.

But for all this ability to reinvent himself, something in Dorian seems to have been fixed as if by a coat of varnish. When we first see him he is very young, even for his age. He pouts and sulks at the prospect of sitting still. He is docile in listening to Lord Henry and absorbing ideas, which he then repeats in similar language like a good child. Then just after he has uttered his wish, he throws a full-blown tantrum. Basil, already aware that his love is not requited, tells Lord Henry, 'Now and then … he is horribly thoughtless, and seems to take a real delight in giving me pain' (p. 13). This is not adult sadism but a child's awareness of its power over someone who loves it.

 **CHECK THE POEM**
The positive aspects of Dorian's love of role-play and shifting identity can be summed up in *Song of Myself* (1891) by Wilde's contemporary, Walt Whitman: 'Do I contradict myself? / Very well then I contradict myself, / (I am large, I contain multitudes)', stanza 51.

**CONTEXT**

Wilde had a number of close Jewish friends, including the actress Ada Leverson, the 'Sphinx' with whom he stayed between his trials and with whom he had corresponded about the reception of *Dorian Gray*. Anti-Semitism was still common, but the Prince of Wales had rendered it less acceptable in polite society than it had been. The anti-Semitism here is like the class arrogance Dorian displays in Chapter 19, a measure of his failure to transcend social boundaries.

There is something of the two-year-old in Dorian, and there never comes a point when he must, like any toddler, deal with the pain of being thwarted. Virtually everyone does what he wants, because his power is sufficient to charm or to blackmail. It is not until the end that he contemplates the notion of denying himself. For 'sparing' Hetty he expects, like a child, to receive some kind of instant gratification with a visible change in the picture. It does not occur to him that at this point virtue has become just another mask to try on.

Virtue is only possible when it springs from an awareness beyond the self. As Lord Henry points out, Dorian has not considered how Hetty will feel about being 'spared'. Dorian never manages this awareness. He can feel pity – for Alan Campbell, for instance – but never empathy. Even when in love, he considers that 'the only thing worth loving is an actress' (p. 43). He thinks about Sibyl's art in terms of how he feels about it rather than how Sibyl achieves what she does, assuming that he can become part of it by engaging in a power struggle with 'the Jew' (p. 46) who manages her. He knows the exact details of her contract and plans to establish her in the West End to reflect glory upon himself. As he tells her, 'the world would have worshipped you, and you would have borne my name' (p. 71). This fits oddly with the fact that Sibyl does not know his name.

Dorian lacks the capacity for self-giving. It is as if Sibyl is the first object in his collection of wonderful things; one would not expect a piece of embroidery to ask one's name. Later, Dorian complains to Lord Henry that he has lost the capacity to love at all, 'lost the passion, and forgotten the desire' (p. 161). He links this to the fact that 'my own personality has become a burden to me' (p. 162).

Dorian is perceived by Basil as someone uniquely gifted, whose charisma offers a freshness of vision and the key to a new, subversive style of painting. To Lord Henry, he embodies the individual who might renew the whole world by his ability to 'live out his life fully and completely' (p. 18). The magic of the picture would seem to have given him the opportunity to realise these possibilities, but it has also locked him in a trap. His story is often likened to that of the Fall. However, Adam and Eve fell into knowledge and understanding: as they lost the Garden of Eden, they acquired an awareness of good and evil and the realisation that they were naked. Dorian's fall is into the knowledge of his own power. It is only modified for a moment by vulnerability, the knowledge that 'the life that was to make his soul would mar his body' (pp. 23–4).

Soon, Dorian discovers that his body will never change. He already has what seems to be limitless wealth to shield him from life's other disasters. But invulnerable, he cannot grow. He can try on a series of masks, but he can only extend his knowledge, not his understanding. He never takes on a role so wholeheartedly that he sacrifices his own desires in order to play it. As a dandy, for example, he takes on the externals, dressing beautifully and enjoying the identity of stylistic role model, but he does not follow through its implications. To be a true dandy is to be in a subversive relationship with a society fixated on money, since it strives for a personal originality that cannot be bought but must come from within. Dorian never challenges the status quo.

Similarly, as a potential Catholic Dorian acts out the rituals of the Mass without 'arresting his intellectual development by any formal acceptance of creed or system' (p. 106). This is creditable in the sense that he thinks for himself, but his ability to commit violence suggests that it is not so much a question of intellectual freedom as picking out only the convenient parts of a creed. His sexual relationships and expeditions into the darker sides of the city are carefully managed. As the text acidly points out, he is 'not really reckless, at any rate in his relations to society' (p. 103). He betrays others to ostracism, poverty and disease, but Dorian's identities of blackmailer, seducer and even murderer do not lead him to confront what he is becoming. Whole books have been written about what it means to kill – Dostoyevsky's *Crime and Punishment* (1866) shows a man dramatically changing as he struggles with the implications of the murder he has committed. Dorian feels terror, but not remorse. The terrible visions he experiences towards the end do not move him to focus for long on his victims. He is afraid that his conscience will torment him with nightmares all his life, but never really considers that this might be his just reward.

> **CONTEXT**
>
> Dorian has a near contemporary and counterpart in children's literature, the title character in J. M. Barrie's *Peter Pan*, first staged in 1904. In his own world, Neverland, Peter plays a series of roles, from Indian chief to father of the Lost Boys, but he refuses 'ever to be a man', and the female characters are constantly frustrated by his lack of response to them. He also denies that there is such a thing as maternal love. However, he still gazes in through the nursery window at other children with their mothers. This is 'the one joy from which he must be forever debarred'. Peter has terrible nightmares, which Barrie's stage directions ascribe to 'the riddle of his being'.

The roles of 'murderer' and 'blackmailer' are not so very different from the historical identities Dorian takes on, like those of the more corrupt and murderous of the Roman emperors. He even dresses up as other people, attending a costume ball as Anne de Joyeuse, the male lover of Henri III, who at his wedding was dressed in bejewelled clothing to make him look exactly like the king. The beguiling prose of the text allows the reader a refreshing break into the minds of these new and bizarre characters. Dorian, however, does not enter into their mentalities but rather sees them as reflections of his own. Even his ancestors interest him primarily in terms of what he may have taken from them. He is confident that he has inherited his mother's looks and love of beauty, but, extraordinarily, does not seem interested in whether she loved him. She is just another mirror: 'the whole of history was merely the record of his own life' (p. 115).

Dorian acts like a collector towards his experiences, whether he has enjoyed them in his imagination, or they have involved real relationships or even crimes. They are like the jewels and embroideries he assembles in great numbers and at unimaginable expense. As he tells Basil, 'I don't want to be at the mercy of my emotions. I want to use them, to enjoy them, and to dominate them' (p. 88). Such conspicuous psychological consumption, however, has a deadening effect. All he can do is repeat his experiences, take more lovers, take more drugs. He still flirts and uses his charm, but it becomes a front to conceal the fate of Basil and hide from James Vane rather than enjoyment of the mask of manners.

Rather than Dorian growing more discerning, his sensibility coarsens. He calls Hetty, his last 'love', 'wonderfully like Sibyl Vane' (p. 167), although they have so little in common that it seems women are becoming a blur to him. He seeks out the ugliness of the slums because beauty lacks the capacity to stir him.

Wilde's comment 'Not "Forgive us our sins" but "Smite us for our iniquities" should be the prayer of a man to a most just God' (p. 174) is not pious moralising, but a recognition that in a world free of personal consequences we remain morally immature. It is not really possible to talk of the 'real' Dorian: he exists as a series of

**CHECK THE FILM**

In Harold Ramis's 1993 movie *Groundhog Day*, Bill Murray plays a broadcaster who lives the same day over and over again. Realising that nothing he does will have any consequences, he overeats, hits people, tries to seduce his producer and makes a number of suicide attempts. Only when he starts to do selfless acts does ordinary time begin again.

performances. Beneath them is a mass of drives, desires and terrors whirling in a void. The 'reality' of Dorian lies in what he does, rather than what he is, and the picture records every action without mercy.

## SIBYL VANE

Sibyl Vane, a young actress and Dorian's first love, lives through a story that is a cliché of the kind of **melodrama** acted by her mother – innocent girl destroyed by aristocratic seducer. But her fierce, although never articulated, intellectual conviction about the power of art makes her Lord Henry's most powerful opponent in the debate about art that runs through the book. As Dorian tells Lord Henry, 'Your voice and the voice of Sibyl Vane are two things that I shall never forget. When I close my eyes, I hear them, and each of them says something different. I don't know which to follow' (pp. 42–3).

Sibyl sees the role of art and imagination as that of making life bearable. She deals with her parting from her brother James, for example, with improvised fantasies about his successful future, mostly taken from melodrama. On stage she makes the fictional real. She takes on the personalities of Shakespeare's women and brings them alive, and in doing so, Basil suggests, she can transform her audience, 'strip them of their selfishness and lend them tears for sorrows that are not their own' (p. 66). The heroines she plays embody aspects of love: Cordelia, dead for loyalty to her father; Imogen and Desdemona, faithful to jealous husbands; Juliet, the tragic personification of true love; and the joyous wits, Portia, Rosalind and Beatrice.

Sibyl's body conveys her thoughts. Her eyes reflect the 'mist' of the dream in her head (p. 50), she interacts spontaneously with her family, touching and hugging on impulse, and is only frustrated when she cannot 'communicate her joy' (p. 56).

Dorian understands Sibyl's 'Prince Charming' fantasy as evidence that she sees him as 'a person in a play' (p. 45), but he fails to understand what this means to her. Love is a risk she deliberately chooses in the face of common sense. She sees 'Prince Charming' as above her, not because of his social status but because he embodies 'what Love himself should be' (p. 51). Her love has a democratic

> **CONTEXT**
>
> Wilde claimed to Herbert Beerbohm Tree, who created the role of Lord Illingworth in *A Woman of No Importance*, that he had taken the plot (about an aristocratic seducer and a poor young girl) from *The Family Herald*, 'which took it – wisely I feel – from my novel *The Picture of Dorian Gray*' (Ellmann, p. 359).

**CONTEXT**

Sibyl's looks are modelled on those of Wilde's wife Constance, whom Wilde described as 'a grave, slight, violet-eyed little Artemis, with great coils of heavy brown hair that make her flower-like head droop like a blossom, and wonderful ivory hands which draw music from the piano so sweet that the birds stop singing to listen' (Ellmann, p. 232).

basis. Sibyl anticipates no problems about money or social mobility, but takes for granted – as Juliet does – that love means marriage between those who love equally. She seems to retain the possibility of economic independence, never saying that she will give up the stage. Rather, she anticipates with excitement playing Juliet before the man she will marry.

Sibyl's bad performance surprises her. When, however, she discusses it – treating Dorian as an equal who will understand, not someone she has to placate – she understands it as a sign of personal growth. Just as the portrait awakened a new consciousness of self in Dorian, so love opens up for Sibyl a gap between what she feels and what she expresses as an artist. Instead of unselfconscious identification with the loves of Rosalind or Beatrice, she experiences a 'passion … that burns me like fire' (p. 70), which can be expressed to Dorian alone. He has awakened her as 'Prince Charming' wakes the Sleeping Beauty, to a new life.

In this new state of being, however, Sibyl is vulnerable. She cannot explain it to Dorian in words he can understand. Her 'voice', that seemed to offer him a different path to follow, cannot convince him that she is now more than 'a pretty face' (p. 71). But there is no way back; her promises that she will 'try to improve' are as desperate and unconvincing as Dorian's resolutions to make his portrait change back to its old beauty. When Dorian says that she has 'passed again into the sphere of art' (p. 88), he is deceiving himself. Love has taken her talent. Loss of love denies her any outlet for her new consciousness. Her suicide is not a last piece of theatre, or an index of weakness, but a recognition that she has lost both love and art and there is nothing left. Sibyl's self has been obliterated, just like Basil's, and her fate as a body on a mortuary slab anticipates his.

## MRS VANE

Mrs Vane provides an image of what Sibyl might have become if she had lived on after the loss of her talent. While her daughter does not wish to 'mimic a passion' (p. 70) she does not feel, Mrs Vane does little else. She lives behind a thick layer of make-up and uses 'those false theatrical gestures that so often become a mode of second nature to a stage-player' (p. 51). This is not because she wishes to deceive, but because, while Sibyl's body reflects the spontaneous thoughts that arise in her mind, her own body and her mind are equally shaped by the second-rate **melodrama** from which she earns her living. Mrs Vane cannot help envisaging the effect her words and gestures have on 'an imaginary gallery' (p. 53) and arranges her family into appropriate melodramatic **tableaux**. The expressions of real affection that might empower and unite the Vanes take on a false and vulgar note that enrages her son James.

To some extent at least Mrs Vane believes in the Cinderella story she has constructed around Sibyl. To her, 'Prince Charming' is obviously an aristocrat, and a catch for her daughter. She resents it when James refuses to play along with this fantasy, but she is also aware of some ugly realities. Realising that they cannot exist without money, she is torn between insisting on loyalty to Mr Isaacs who has 'advanced us fifty pounds' (p. 50) (for what, exactly, we do not know) and holding out for an alliance with a rich 'Prince Charming'.

Mrs Vane is also aware that Sibyl is in danger of repeating her own mistakes. While the mother's story has taken on the colouring of melodrama – she cannot help enjoying the situation James creates by demanding to know his parentage and would like to prolong it – its reality is genuinely painful. She has loved a man, 'highly connected' (p. 58) and not free to marry, had a relationship with him long and serious enough result in two children, and he has died. She has clearly endured not just financial hardship but also contempt as a result. The memory is painful and she feels a 'hideous sense of humiliation' (p. 58) when pressed to discuss her story. Her defence is that, as an orphan, she had no one to protect her, as she imagines she is protecting Sibyl. Perhaps, though, she knows that she cannot speak to her about her situation in a language sufficiently direct and simple; she is certainly glad of James's melodramatic reassurance that he will not allow any wrong to Sibyl to go unpunished. Her inability to shed the theatrical not only indicates that she is less intelligent and gifted than her daughter. It also reveals her as the product of exhaustion and the strains of a hard life that has left her 'a faded, tired-looking woman' (p. 50), with thin white hands and a 'withered cheek' (p. 53).

 **CHECK THE BOOK**

William Archer's book *Masks or Faces?*, first published in 1888, is an exploration by a noted critic and playwright of the experience of performers and the ways that they share, or fail to share, the emotions of the characters they play.

## JAMES VANE

Sibyl's brother James, a sailor, lives in a state of reaction against falsehood, which to him is symbolised by the theatre. He despises his mother's posturing and avoids giving her too many opportunities for it, and he is determined to take his sister 'off the stage' (p. 52) despite her delight in acting. He pushes his mother into uncomfortable admissions about his paternity, a matter on which he has brooded for a long time. He asserts his perfectly reasonable right to the truth, but he is also 'enraged' (p. 58) by her emotional response and it seems that he has to hurt her before he can feel pity.

James's mother had hoped that he might enter a profession. This may not be an unrealistic sentiment as he seems to have the necessary intelligence, and perhaps Mr Isaac's money was destined to make it possible. The young man's choice of a seafaring life is a clear one, based on his hatred of 'offices, and … clerks' (p. 52), which seems to spring from his strong sense of class oppression.

The loathing James feels for Dorian as a 'gentleman' is instinctive – although his sense that Dorian wants to 'enslave' (p. 56) Sibyl has a base in reason. So, too, does his dislike of Dorian as a 'young dandy' (p. 54) – that is, as someone playing a role, as false in his way as Mrs Vane. However, jealousy forms a part of his hatred, and James never acknowledges this. Nor does he acknowledge that there is a **melodramatic** aspect to the threats he utters to 'track him down and kill him like a dog' (p. 58).

James does his best to keep his word – just like a sailor-hero of popular drama. However, in melodrama, the young working-class male who stands up to the aristocrat exposes the latter's lies and corruption before defeating him. James misses his chance by allowing Dorian's youthful face to deceive him, and his essential decency leads him to tremble at the idea that he might have killed an innocent man. However, the way that he crumbles into deference with a 'Forgive me, sir' (p. 151) seems a long way from the young would-be avenger of eighteen years ago, and all the more **ironic** in that he is killed by one of the most worthless members of a class he so despises.

**QUESTION**

Is betrayal the real unforgivable sin in the novel?

## VICTORIA WOTTON

Lord Henry's wife has something in common with Mrs Vane in that her life is a series of roles which she does not always manage to bring off. In the world of upper-class erotic intrigue, she is 'usually in love with somebody' (p. 38) – unrequitedly but evidently enjoyably. According to Lord Henry, the two of them are engaged in a process of continual deception.

Victoria is nervous and chaotic, her clothes and conversation both compiled of odds and ends. However, there is a charm in this image of 'a bird of paradise that had been out all night in the rain' (p. 39). Lord Henry clearly neglects her – she complains that she only hears of his views from his friends – but she seems to understand him better than he thinks, and it is not surprising that he misses her when she is gone. Running away with a pianist is not done in this world of polite sexual hypocrisy. Victoria does not seem to have suffered for it, as Dorian's victims do. In her slightly eccentric way, she offers a bolder challenge to the status quo than any of the men.

## LADY NARBOROUGH

Of all the characters in the novel, this old lady is perhaps the most contented with her lot. She is not beautiful and her life has been spent making the best of a marriage with a dull man who has given her dull children. She has remained a faithful wife, an efficient parent – at least in marrying off her daughters – and a good diplomatic hostess. She is highly educated and her intelligence allows her to play her social role well.

Lady Narborough flirts elegantly, telling Dorian that she is 'jealous' (p. 140) of his affection. But she always deftly returns the conversation to the subject of her age, making it clear that the game is no more than a game.

## THE DUCHESS OF MONMOUTH

If Lady Narborough is an example of how to make the best of the restrictive situation of the upper-class nineteenth-century woman, the young and pretty Duchess of Monmouth seems about to exemplify the opposite. She is enthralled by Dorian, and profoundly

**QUESTION**

How do the opportunities open to the female characters compare to those of the men in *Dorian Gray*?

THE DUCHESS OF MONMOUTH continued

bored by her husband, a dull sixty-year-old whose main interest is beetles. She admits that the 'strawberry leaves' (p. 163), the sign of his peerage, were his only attraction and are the reason she stays with him. However, she does not share Lady Narborough's sense of obligation to be faithful to her marriage bargain (p. 163).

Lord Henry describes the Duchess as 'very clever' (p. 144). She is clearly politically aware, a committed Tory and social Darwinist, and there is some resentment in her accusation that Dorian finds her 'a modern butterfly' (p. 155). Her repartee is sparkling, but she does not seem to get the pleasure that Lady Narborough does from wit and flirtation for their own sake. Rather, they are a **subtext** through which she declares her desire for Dorian. Eventually she abandons it to make what seems to be an overt invitation. She wins a compliment about Artemis, goddess of the hunt – which suggests that she may look too predatory for her own good.

The shooting of James Vane postpones what promises to be a dangerous affair. The men's diagnosis – that Dorian likes without loving, while the Duchess loves without liking – appears accurate. It seems that, nevertheless, the Duchess eventually takes the risk, and pays the price of loss. By the time Dorian makes his resolution to be 'good' he has abandoned her.

Lord Henry's remark that 'her clever tongue gets on one's nerves' (p. 173) may indicate that she has lost her wit, but it may simply reflect her situation as a woman with no real outlet for her intelligence. The Duchess has, though, been intelligent enough to retain her social position, unlike other aristocratic victims of Dorian's beauty.

## ALAN CAMPBELL

Alan Campbell is the male equivalent of Sibyl Vane: brilliantly talented and finally destroyed. Of all Dorian's male victims, he seems most in control of his own destiny. We learn that he has the energy and ability to make himself into a noted chemist against the wishes of a more conventional family. He bonds with Dorian over the music that they both enjoy and play to a high standard, and

**CONTEXT**

The word 'blackmail' comes from the word for 'tribute' (protection money) paid by English and Scottish border dwellers to the Border Reivers, or Freebooters, in return for immunity from raids and violence. This *reditus nigri*, 'black rent' (or 'black mail'), was paid in goods and labour, whereas *reditus albi*, 'white rent', was paid in silver. Blackmail – over sexual or financial misconduct – was a common theme in Victorian literature, and features in Wilde's play *An Ideal Husband*.

their relationship at its peak is one of literal and metaphorical harmony. What changes the relationship is not revealed, but we are told that to Alan 'Dorian Gray was the type of everything that is wonderful and fascinating in life' (p. 132). This suggests that the power was in the hands of Dorian, whose feelings are never revealed.

Unlike some of Dorian's lovers, Alan has inner resources. He clearly gains strength from science, which now fills his life. **Ironically**, this means that he is exactly what Dorian needs after the murder. Dorian breaks him completely with his blackmailing letter: the idea of disgrace affects him with the sense of physical torture. Despite the cold and stern words with which he takes apparent control of the situation, dismissing Dorian from the room and taking an initiative in refusing to see him again, Alan feels 'dominated' (p. 137) by Dorian. It may be that he cannot break Dorian's hold, or that he is ashamed of what he has done. His suicide does not come as a surprise. Tragically, he chooses his laboratory as the setting for his own death.

## ADRIAN SINGLETON

Adrian Singleton represents a whole group of young men who are disgraced when they fall under Dorian's sway. In his case the sin committed against society is financial, the forging of a friend's name on a bill. The upper class was unforgiving of such misdemeanours, even if they had no serious consequences for the wealthy victims.

Adrian is rescued from debt, but his social ostracism is permanent. Opium is a substitute for the world he has lost: 'As long as one has this stuff, one doesn't want friends' (p. 148), he tells Dorian. It drains him of the will to want anything better.

His yellow hair makes him one of the many mirrors Dorian encounters in the text. This is the person that Dorian might be without the protection of his wealth and beauty. He is also a mirror of Alan Campbell. Despite strength of will and talent on the one hand and idle passivity on the other, both are turned into the shells of their former selves by Dorian.

> **CONTEXT**
>
> Words like 'musical' or 'artistic' were often used in the nineteenth century as a way of implying that a man was homosexual, and the references to the shared interest in music are in part a way of coding the relationship between Dorian and Alan as homosexual. They also, of course, symbolise harmony and happiness, and Alan's abandonment of music is a sign that he is not at peace with himself.

# THEMES

## LONDON

When Dorian speaks of 'this grey, monstrous London of ours, with its myriads of people, its sordid sinners, and its splendid sins' (p. 41), he expresses the ambivalent relationship of British Victorians to their capital. The idea of the city gripped the nineteenth-century imagination, and London was the biggest and most powerful city on earth.

As the century wore on, literature showed a place divided: the rich, whether from inherited wealth or burgeoning industrialisation, inhabited the West End; the East End, once associated with a respectable if modestly paid working class, was now 'Darkest England', as General Booth of the Salvation Army called it, filled with criminals and a desperate and diseased poor on the brink of revolution.

It is still possible to walk the streets of Dorian's London: virtually every place mentioned is in the A–Z handbook, although the first thing to strike you is that there are so many places Wilde does not mention at all. To take the novel as a guide to London is to miss the middle-class suburbs, department stores and ordinary homes. For the London of this tale is an image of Dorian's own divided nature: he embodies the best and the worst of the society in which he lives.

Dorian is what the age called a *flâneur* – a wealthy wanderer who spends his time, as Walter Benjamin puts it, 'botanizing on the asphalt', observing the life of the streets like a scientist (*Charles Baudelaire: A Lyric Poet in the Era of High Capitalism*, 1983, p. 36). This also involves being observed. The streets are a set on which the *flâneur* displays himself or melts into the crowd at will. He crosses borderlands between social extremes.

Sibyl's theatre is on the border of the East. It is a place where a rich man can be a spectacle for others – Dorian sits rigidly in his box, while the disappointed audience boo – or can, like Basil, take pleasure in the sight of the inhabitants, the 'tawdry girls' and the young men who take off their jackets and eat oranges in the packed galleries under an

**CHECK THE BOOK**

Peter Ackroyd's *London: The Biography* is a vivid account of the city's history, organised by theme rather than chronology. It explores in detail the East–West divide.

**CHECK THE BOOK**

Judith Walkowitz's *City of Dreadful Delight* is a study of late nineteenth-century London as it concerned women, examining the evidence of the social reformers who traversed the slums, the women threatened by the Whitechapel murders of Jack the Ripper and the newly emancipated women walking the streets and browsing its department stores.

artificial sun. Covent Garden market forms the border of the West, an unexpectedly rural oasis with cart-horses and men in white smocks. Loaded with flowers to sell, they defer to the wealthy who are walking home from a night on the town. Dorian is given cherries to eat as if it is his right as a gentleman: nobody asks him to pay.

Birth grants access to a rigidly exclusive London. Dorian lives in Grosvenor Square, then as now an address with great prestige. His 'oak-panelled hall of entrance', lit by a lantern that is the 'spoil of some Doge's barge' (p. 72), is a visual sign of power and ownership. One would expect the servants to control entry as rigidly as Francis, Victor and the rest do when not traversing the length and breadth of London in search of orchids, furniture movers or whatever is needed. It is significant that other classes feel inhibited by this exclusive world, even when they have a perfect right to the space. James Vane remarks that only 'swell people' (p. 52) can walk in Hyde Park, and he and Sibyl strain to see 'Prince Charming' drive by in his carriage, part of a parade of Dukes and 'smart people' who attract a 'crowd of watchers' (p. 56).

The interiors inhabited by the rich are carefully described. Lord Henry decorates his library in a style Wilde favoured for his own house. Dorian's bedroom has 'olive-satin curtains' lined with 'shimmering blue' (p. 76). Such detail does not merely make the settings more vivid but shows the endless possibilities for choice available to the wealthy. However, these choices are controlled by a fierce social network which may deny access to privileged space altogether if the rules are flouted. Early in the **narrative** Lord Henry's sister has a box at the opera at her disposal; later, when she is socially disgraced, her territory shrinks. Basil reproaches Dorian, 'Is there a single decent woman in London now who would drive with her in the Park?' (p. 120).

The inhabitants of the East End have little access to the grander parts of the West, except as workers. (Some, of course, are almost starving because they have no work.) People like the Vane family, or the cab driver who does not want to take Dorian to a location as rough as Bluegate Fields, cling to a perilous respectability. Sibyl's family own a single armchair, a modest status symbol.

**CHECK THE BOOK**

A classic text on the real London of the period is Henry Mayhew's *London Labour and the London Poor*, published in 1861 (republished 1968 by Dover Books).

LONDON continued

**CHECK THE BOOK**

One of the earliest nineteenth-century novelists to explore the theme of the double was James Hogg, whose *Confessions of a Justified Sinner* (1824) tells the story of a puritanically reared young man eaten up with resentment of his likeable and legitimate brother. He encounters a mysterious figure called Gil-Martin, who persuades him that, as one of God's elect, nothing he does is a sin. A career of murder and betrayal follows. Finally, he commits suicide. The story leaves it ambiguous whether Gil-Martin is the devil or a figment of the young man's imagination.

Dorian, however, has the freedom of the East End, as one of the wealthy *flâneurs* who liked to go 'slumming' on a regular basis. He is an experienced thrill-seeker who knows where opium is to be found, the differences in quality from house to house, and who is likely to be in those houses. (Most real opium houses were actually far cleaner than the sordid dens described here. They had their share of wealthy young Londoners; one Limehouse resident noted that many of the 'slummers' had to give up smoking opium because they couldn't manage to keep their pipes alight (Berridge, p. 205).)

Dorian's East End is not just a geographical location but a state of mind. The Gothic novel of the early nineteenth century dealt in graveyards and ruined castles as a backdrop for its vampires and **villains**. Now Dorian, like Dracula draining people of life and hope, descends into a kind of urban Hell, its 'lonely brickfields' and 'strange bottle-shaped kilns with the orange fan-like tongues of fire' (p. 147) lit by a 'moon … like a yellow skull' (p. 146). He does not merely melt into the crowd like a man-about-town observing life: he vanishes into a London fog, the natural habitat of criminals in the pages of Conan Doyle.

This London eventually becomes for Dorian a truer reality than his own world of art and privilege. The 'coarse brawl, the loathsome den, the crude violence' (p. 147) provide an intensity of experience that allows him to forget his personal terrors. However, they also remind the reader that the ugly face of poverty shown here was a reality, one to be feared if no social change was forthcoming.

## THE DOUBLE

The idea that we have another 'self', that we are not a single identity with clear boundaries, is a disturbing one that literature has explored for generations. Sometimes all ends happily and the second 'self' is merely a long-lost sibling, as in Wilde's own *The Importance of Being Earnest.* Often, though, the figure of the *doppelganger* ('double-goer') remains terrifying, at once familiar, undermining our sense of uniqueness, but also alien, suggesting aspects of ourselves that we do not know, even violently acting out repressed desires.

Dorian's relationship with his *doppelganger*, the painting, is complex. At first he imagines that it will teach him about himself: 'the most magical of mirrors. As it had revealed to him his own body, so it would reveal to him his own soul' (p. 86). Significantly, he hides it in a schoolroom. Even as he does so, however, he is reflecting on its advantages for his body, with which he is already, thanks to the portrait, in love.

The magical Other becomes the key to a double life. As the contrast between them grows, it is a source of 'terrible delight' (p. 103). But the division between body and soul is not as straightforward as Dorian imagines. The painting records and reflects both his internal and his external reality, but it cannot feel. Meanwhile Dorian, too, loses this capacity. He is not shocked but merely 'interested' (p. 103) in the corruption in his portrait, and feels 'pity' for his soul – an emotion the text labels 'purely selfish' (p. 103).

Wilde's original submission to *Lippincott's* was 'The Fisherman and his Soul', the story of a man who gives away his soul to win the love of a mermaid. The soul has many adventures, but becomes criminal and cruel. It pleads to return, but only when the mermaid dies and the fisherman's heart breaks can the soul re-enter. Dorian's motive for splitting soul and body is based on love for himself, not another, and in the process something is lost. He revels in the idea that 'we can multiply our personalities' (p. 113) through the playful and insincere formalities of polite society which he performs with sparkling charm, but he can hardly be sincere given that he is a living mask whose true face is in the attic.

Throughout the story Dorian is confronted with mirror images of himself, or acts as a mirror to others. Basil tries constantly to present Dorian with the image of the virtuous man he might be, even inviting him to copy him in kneeling in prayer as he sees the horror of the picture. The sensual Dorian is consciously mirroring the hero of the book given to him by Lord Henry, except that while the 'wonderful young Parisian' came to dread mirrors, it is only his image in the picture that Dorian fears. While Lord Henry himself attends parties and utters witty lines, Dorian acts out the 'fiery-coloured life' (p. 49) that Lord Henry dare not risk, a mirror of his desire.

**CHECK THE BOOK**

In J. K. Rowling's Harry Potter series, the evil Lord Voldemort has split his soul into seven pieces by committing seven murders, and has lodged the pieces in seven magical objects known as Horcruxes. Only if these are destroyed can he be killed. Similarly, Dorian is immortal as long as his picture is safe.

**CHECK THE BOOK**

An accessible study of the topic can be found in Robert Rogers's *The Double in Literature* (1970).

**CHECK
THE BOOK**

For our century, the idea of the double is often explored in fictions about cloning. For example, Caryl Churchill's play *A Number*, in 2002, showed a man confronted not only with the son he had abandoned as unsatisfactory, but the clone he had had made to start parenthood afresh and a clone made without his knowledge.

The people Dorian destroys are also images of what he might have been in different circumstances: Sibyl Vane, with her beauty and talent but lacking the power he derives from his gender, his status and his portrait; Adrian Singleton and Alan Campbell, both golden boys who disintegrate because they lack his magical immunity.

Though Dorian can accept or reject all these mirrors at will, he fails to realise that he cannot survive without his double. He sees the portrait as having a twin role. It is his 'conscience', showing him the blood on his hands, seeming to urge him to confess, but it is also the 'one bit of evidence left against him' (p. 176) when all traces of the murder of Basil have been obliterated. Dorian thinks that by destroying the evidence he will also be free of the inner voice that tells him to confess. But the double is a powerful entity, and every story of doubles makes it clear that eventually it has to be confronted. It can destroy, but not be destroyed. And it cannot be ignored.

## ART

You begin to understand the complexity of the questions that the novel asks about art when you try to imagine the portrait itself. If you stand in front of a mirror and try to give your mouth 'the curved wrinkle of the hypocrite' (p. 176) you realise that it is impossible. The whole point about hypocrisy is that it looks fine on the surface. The newspapers show the faces of people guilty of terrible crimes, but they do not look different from the rest of us.

The painting shows something about Dorian that is true, but not 'real', in the sense that it shows what Dorian *would* look like if he had never prayed that he and the picture could change places. It is the reader's role to co-operate with the text in imagining the portrait by considering some of the ideas embodied in the text, but no two readers' images will be the same.

A debate about art, illusion and reality runs through the story, although it is never formalised into discussion. When Basil talks about 'a dream of form in days of thought' (p. 12), he is alluding to an idea familiar to classically educated Victorians: Plato's 'Theory of Forms'. This states that earthly life is filled with imperfect copies of a divine reality and that the perfect 'form' – whether it be a table, a horse, or a relationship – exists in another plane.

Plato felt that art could only copy the copies. Many artists considered the reverse to be true, believing that art came *closer* to showing the divine perfection. Sibyl seems to agree with Plato: she finds that acting Juliet is such a pale reflection of the reality of love that she can no longer bear to do it. Basil seems to have a more complex position. Looking at the picture, he tells Dorian 'yes, you are just like that' (p. 27). But he has also painted his own adoration into the canvas. Lovers tend to have a very idealised image of the beloved. When Basil calls the picture 'the real Dorian' (p. 26), he may mean that he has shown a Dorian better than the one currently rejecting him to go to the theatre with Lord Henry.

We can learn something about the special 'reality' of the portrait through an understanding of Victorian style. Basil is young, radical – as implied by Lord Henry's suggestion of the Grosvenor Gallery – and on the edge of a great leap forward. His earlier work suggests that he shares the interests of the Pre-Raphaelites, who favoured literary, historical or mythological subjects familiar to their public. They liked to show a life-changing event, a frozen moment of decision. Basil paints Dorian as Antinoüs, sailing on the Nile and possibly contemplating the moment when he will sacrifice himself to the river. He also shows him as Paris, 'in dainty armour' (p. 92), the prince who stole Helen of Troy from her husband; and as Adonis, the hunter who rejects a goddess. In these images Dorian is given a glimpse of possible lives: he has not yet chosen one for himself. Dorian also models as Narcissus, gazing at his reflection in the water – a kind of dress rehearsal for the final portrait. The portrait shows Dorian 'realistically' in that he is in ordinary clothes, with no role to play and no costume to help him imagine that he is someone else. In this sense it acts as Narcissus's pool, an image that will trap him in fatal self-love.

Basil has entered his own picture. He sees his feelings in 'every flake and film' of it (p. 92). He tells Lord Henry that any work painted with such passion 'is a portrait of the artist, not of the sitter' (p. 8). The tragedy of the story is that, blinded by the 'realism' of the

**CONTEXT**

The innovative nature of Basil's ideas are borne out by Lord Henry's suggestion of the avant-garde Grosvenor Gallery, favoured by the most challenging artists of the day, as a venue for the painting. Wilde wrote a review in the *Dublin University Magazine* praising the Grosvenor, where Whistler and the Pre-Raphaelites featured strongly, when it opened in 1877. In Gilbert and Sullivan's comic opera *Patience* (see **Oscar Wilde's life and works**), the hero, Bunthorne, a caricature of Wilde, is called a 'greenery-yallery, Grosvenor-Gallery, foot-in-the-grave young man'.

ART continued

**CONTEXT**

Wilde's prose poem 'The Disciple' tells the story of the pool that reflected Narcissus and how it wept at his death. The nymphs try to comfort it, saying, 'We do not wonder that you should mourn in this manner for Narcissus, so beautiful was he.' The pool answers, 'But I loved Narcissus because, as he lay on my banks and looked down on me, in the mirror of his eyes I saw my own beauty mirrored' (Holland, p. 844).

treatment, Dorian cannot see this. He cannot see Basil's love informing 'every flake and film' any more than Narcissus can see the surface of the pool on which he is reflected, and he takes the image not as a lover's idealisation but as the revelation of a perfection that he really possesses. Dorian chooses to remain in that inhumanly perfect state for ever. The impossible beauty is a fiction that allows him to seduce, to torment and to betray while the picture takes on the task of showing not one moment of decision but the result of every decision he makes.

The beautiful face that belies the exploitation and violence within has a social as well as an individual aspect. The story takes place at a crucial moment in the nineteenth century as art was opening up to the people. When the Pre-Raphaelites had a difficult reception from the art establishment of their own day, they turned to galleries in the industrial north, such as those in Manchester and Liverpool, implicitly inviting the public to make up their own minds. This democratisation of art was supported by new techniques of reproduction, such as lithography and photography. The Marxist critic Walter Benjamin (1892–1940) suggested that this constituted a political crossroads.

The unique 'aura' of a work of art once gave it a magical significance, linked to specifically religious ritual and later to the idea of beauty. Responses were shaped by those, whether priests or art experts, who revealed it to the privileged spectator. The arrival of the cheap reproduction made possible a different kind of response. The middle-class patrons of the provincial galleries and the working-class householders with a few pence to spare to decorate their walls with cheap reproductions had a 'sense of the universal equality of things' (Benjamin, p. 225). When Basil enthusiastically decides to exhibit, he is making it possible for the picture's lithographic reproduction to find its way into every house in the country. The corrupt self that Dorian hides, concealed by wealth and power as well as the magic of the picture, would then become the property of the ordinary citizens, the servants who maintain him and the working-class figures he seduces. Instead, it rots in lonely state beneath a cloth once used in a church; it is ritually revealed by Dorian to himself alone, the image of a corrupt member of a class in decay.

# STRUCTURE AND NARRATIVE

*Dorian Gray* was Wilde's first lengthy prose **narrative**, and he did not find it easy. After the *Lippincott's* version he wrote of feeling tired and dissatisfied: 'I am afraid it is rather like my own life – all conversation and no action' (Ellmann, p. 296). The 1891 version allowed him to incorporate the James Vane revenge plot and develop the **social comedy**. The resulting mixture is, as Richard Ellmann puts it, 'elegantly casual' (Ellmann, p. 297). It seems as if the rules of novel-writing have been torn up, and the reader never knows whether their next experience will be Gothic terror, social satire, a discourse on art or a short account of the more decadent Caesars.

However, underlying the casualness is a solid framework. By 1892 Wilde would complete his first successful **comedy**, *Lady Windermere's Fan*, and the shape to which virtually all Victorian plays conformed is also the basic shape of *Dorian Gray*. The **well-made play**, as it was known, begins with a clear **exposition** which provides the audience with the information they need to understand the action. It goes on to the **development and complication** of the story, raising the level of tension as to how events will resolve themselves. About three-quarters of the way through, the action reaches a **crisis** (in the theatre, just in time for the third act curtain) as the strands of the plot entwine. Matters come to a head with a series of shocks and surprises, and while we know that the end is imminent, we are still in suspense as to how it will happen. The **dénouement** accomplishes it – whether with death or marriage, repentance or revenge, happiness or pathos, will depend on the nature of the play. Wilde may not have been conscious of using the format, but it could explain why *Dorian Gray* has been so frequently dramatised.

The well-made structure happens to fit very closely the narrative stages necessary for the story of the devil's bargain, and virtually every version of the Faustus story conforms to it, even if written in a different convention. The exposition sets up the conditions that explain why the bargain is made – in this case, the chapters which bring together for the first time Basil's adoration, Dorian's

**CHECK THE BOOK**

Karl Beckson's *Oscar Wilde: The Critical Heritage* (1970) is a compendium of critical responses to Wilde's work from 1881 onwards. It usefully charts the way that different eras have responded to the man and how this has affected judgements on his work.

## CONTEXT

In Marlowe's *Doctor Faustus*, the protagonist asks Mephistopheles to give him Helen of Troy for a lover. He gets a devil in her shape. As he kisses her, he says: 'Her lips suck forth my soul – see where it flies.' Faustus does not realise that this is not a poetic fancy but what is actually happening. Intercourse with the devil ensures that he will go to hell.

beauty and Lord Henry's seductive praise of youth. The **development** confirms that the bargain has actually occurred. The section in which Dorian loves and rejects Sibyl also makes it clear that the bargain has consequences for others, not just the **protagonist**, laying the ground for James Vane's role in the outcome. The **complication** explores the extent and meaning of the unholy power acquired. Wilde reveals shifts in Dorian's relationships with Basil, Lord Henry and the world at large, and the relationship with his own image that increasingly governs his actions. Chapter 11 in particular has the scope and sweep that makes the leap over a period of eighteen years credible. We do not know the details of Dorian's sins, but the arrival of Basil in Chapter 12 provokes the **crisis** – in the story of the devil's bargain, the point at which the protagonist may want to escape damnation but commits a sin from which there is no way back.

The murder of Basil shifts this phase of the action into the realm of the detective story. While the portrait may conceal Dorian's debauchery, he is as likely to be hanged for murder as anyone else. All his subsequent actions, from dining in polite society to smoking opium, are some form of mental or physical flight, and even the most leisurely chat seems charged with an underlying speed as Dorian's terror mounts. James Vane brings the strands of the story together, providing not just the suspense of a revenge plot but a modern version of a Gothic haunting. His sudden appearances in different locations are perfectly realistic, but they shock Dorian with the force of an avenging ghost.

Wilde surprises his readers by allowing Dorian to escape all the obvious forms of justice, such as being killed by James Vane. In the legends, the devil himself would provide the **dénouement**, arriving to claim the soul that is owed to him. Here, Dorian does the job himself. His psyche seems to disintegrate in front of us. As in Marlowe's play, it is left to the minor characters, the servants, to pick up the pieces and assert the identity of the remains.

Not only does the plot carry its own structural weight. We also navigate the text through a series of images resembling stage tableaux: Dorian at the piano, young and innocent, and again, playing Chopin to Lord Henry in a very different spirit; Dorian sleeping sweetly after increasingly terrible acts; the combination of Dorian, the painting, a knife, and Basil – in the final repetition represented only by a spreading bloodstain. These freeze-frame moments allow us to evaluate the protagonist as he changes and to re-evaluate our own responses.

## LANGUAGE AND STYLE

Once you have read his essays or stories, or seen one of his plays, or even heard some of his witticisms, you can easily identify the distinctive style of Oscar Wilde. He took enormous pains to polish his work, and drafts of *Dorian Gray* reveal a large number of small alterations that show the attention he paid to the precise choice of words and to the rhythm of his sentences. Brought up in an age and a country which regarded story-telling and reading aloud as valuable accomplishments, he was at pains to make his work easy on the ear.

Wilde's prose varies in tone from sharp and witty one-liners to elaborate, sensuous passages which develop argument but also hypnotise with their distinctive rhythms. Regenia Gagnier has suggested that he developed the first to please the public and the second for a more specialised readership, young and educated (*Idylls of the Marketplace*, p. 4), although *Dorian Gray*, unlike Wilde's critical essays or **social comedies**, is a blend of both. Certainly Wilde is always aware of the presence of his reader and takes pains to shape a lively relationship between reader and writer. The Preface to *Dorian Gray*, signed 'Oscar Wilde', is a direct challenge to us to pay attention and draw our own conclusions about the story.

Wilde was not interested in originality. His work does not surprise with novelties but makes readers look afresh at what they think they already know. We are not encouraged to 'lose ourselves' in a realistic **narrative** that gives us the sense of a narrator reporting what he sees at first hand, but are constantly made aware that this

**CONTEXT**

Some examples of Wilde's attention to fine detail can be seen in earlier versions of the final paragraphs. For instance, the original typescript read 'one of the maids was crying', which Wilde changed to 'Old Mrs Leaf was crying', allowing Dorian one servant who stays throughout his lifetime. In the *Lippincott's* version, the corpse of Dorian wears only one ring.

**CONTEXT**

Some sections of the novel use traditional literary formats. For example, Dorian's meditation on the loss of material things in Chapter 11 – 'Where had they passed to? Where was the great crocus-coloured robe ...' (p. 110) – turns a list of exotic objects drawn from an academic treatise into a lament, a poetic form going back to ancient Rome and known as *Ubi sunt* (where are ...?).

book has been made by a craftsman who is working within literary traditions.

The novel is **intertextual** – that is, it not only quotes other texts but encourages the reader to explore its relationship with them. Dorian reads Gautier's *Enamels and Cameos* to forget the murder he has committed; Lord Henry and Basil quote the King James Bible when they speak of the soul; Sibyl Vane finds that the words of Juliet on her balcony do not express her feelings and chooses instead those of Tennyson's Lady of Shalott. All these texts, especially when they seem to be inappropriate, express something about the speakers that they may be unable to articulate.

Wilde is not assuming, as an eighteenth-century novelist might, that his readers all possess such knowledge. Rather, his text educates them so that they share the perspective of the craftsman-author. This is appropriate to a novel about the effects of art, as it makes the reader hypersensitive to the responsibilities of the artist; and as the knowledge of the ageless Dorian becomes extended, the text extends that of the reader. Even those who shared Wilde's Oxford background and recognised the scraps of French and Latin dotted throughout the text would probably be meeting words like 'orphrey' (p. 11) and 'cymophane' (p. 108) for the first time.

The extension of our own sense experience is also achieved through a characteristic Wilde takes from the work of the Decadents, especially Baudelaire: **synaesthesia,** the use of one sense to interpret another. Hence light is 'shrill' (p. 50) and the perfume of lilacs can be drunk like wine (p. 20). Distant or abstract things take on sensual immediacy: a star's light is 'wan' like a face (p. 101), and Lord Henry can make the company see Philosophy as a woman with bubbles of wine staining her skin (p. 36). The disconcerting effect is not just a stylistic mannerism but prepares us for the confused and shifting perspectives of Dorian as his life begins to fall apart.

At the same time, fleeting and concrete images take on a sudden importance, as if the material world is commenting on the situation. Wilde often moves the **narrative** away from a major character to focus on a detail, as a camera might cut from an actor's face to a symbolic object. As Dorian is listening to Lord Henry for the first time, for instance, the text abruptly shifts focus to a tiny image that an artist might paint: 'A furry bee … began to scramble all over the oval stellated globe of the tiny blossoms' (p. 22). Increasingly these images become threatening, as if Dorian's consciousness can no longer shut out what is happening to him: the flash of a policeman's lantern after the murder; the twitching of an elderly addict who imagines he is covered in red ants.

Wilde could be called an **omniscient narrator** in that he appears able to tell us every aspect of his characters' thoughts. However, his usual method of doing this is to use **free indirect speech**: that is, the thoughts are not reported dispassionately in **indirect speech** ('Dorian thought that Sibyl had let him down by killing herself'); nor are they treated as monologues in **direct speech** ('"Sibyl has let me down," thought Dorian'), which tends to sound false in the absence of a listening audience. Rather, they are narrated in language consistent with the thinker, but in the **third person**, giving an extra distance that invites us not simply to observe but to judge, as we 'hear' what they would never dream of voicing aloud. The passage beginning 'Had he been cruel?' (p. 74) relates Dorian's thought processes about his treatment of Sibyl without comment. Yet as he moves from self-righteousness ('She had been shallow and unworthy') to self-centredness ('During the three terrible hours the play had lasted, he had lived centuries of pain') to smug sexism ('Besides, women were better suited to bear sorrow than men'), he is simultaneously comic in his immaturity and monstrous in his selfishness.

When characters speak aloud, they often do so with the wit for which Wilde was famous. But while these bouts of wit provide a refreshing contrast in pace and tone to the slower prose of their unvoiced thoughts, the jokes are not gratuitous. Dorian moves in the aristocratic world of the 1890s, which operated through powerful but unwritten codes geared to its own preservation. There were topics that could not be discussed (especially those that might undermine political or intellectual stasis), emotions that could not be expressed (especially those not conducive to the preservation of

**CHECK THE BOOK**

In the Preface to his 1895 science fiction novel *The Island of Doctor Moreau* (Phoenix Paperbacks, 2004), H. G. Wells explains that the book was inspired by the Wilde trial – 'a scandalous trial about that time, the graceless and pitiful downfall of a man of genius … this story was the response of an imaginative mind to the reminder that humanity is but animal rough-hewn to a reasonable shape and in perpetual internal conflict between instinct and injunction' (p. 121), shows how Wells valued the sophisticated use of language by men like Wilde as an index of civilisation.

**CONTEXT**

As Regina Gagnier points out of Wilde's own wit, the mockery is 'on, and with, its own terms. The use of such tactics endear the speaker to the group' (Gagnier, p. 8).

**QUESTION**

What does the dialogue show about relationships between different classes or genders in Victorian England?

**CONTEXT**

Tartuffe is the protagonist of Molière's 1664 comedy. Pretending to be a religious man, he indulges in all kinds of gluttony, lechery and exploitation. He is said here to have 'opened a shop', making a reference to Napoleon's famous description of the English as 'a nation of shopkeepers'.

the high-born family with a man at its head), and formalities that had to be preserved, however trying the circumstances (such as the presence of anyone who did not know the code or refused to adhere to it). Sincerity was not as important as playing your social part well.

For some of the powerful it is enough to utter **clichés**, like Lord Fermor's 'Young people, nowadays, imagine that money is everything' (p. 28). The function of such remarks is to assert the social or even political authority of the speaker rather than advance an argument – in his description of the tedious Chapman, Wilde calls it 'hoist[ing] the Union Jack on the pinnacles of Thought' (p. 143). Invariably, though, they speak with perfect grammar and in complete sentences: this is not a world where anyone is interrupted by an idea or a passion breaking in. Others prefer to show authority through wit which inverts the clichés, such as Lord Henry's 'Moderation is a fatal thing. Enough is as bad as a meal. More than enough is as good as a feast' (p. 143). This generates laughter, and may even make the reader pause to think, but it is also a way of asserting the speaker's own control over the code of the exclusive circle.

Even the sharpest observations are articulated in a way that underlines their entertainment value, like this interlude between Lord Henry and the Duchess:

'What did they say of us?'

'That Tartuffe has emigrated to England and opened a shop.'

'Is that yours, Harry?'

'I give it to you.' (p. 154)

Tartuffe, Molière's archetypal religious hypocrite, is an appropriate **metaphor** for a society capable of bullying Dorian's sexual conquests (such as Lord Henry's sister) merely for being found out. Here, however, the point is not to have a political discussion, but to use the language of politics for a display of vivacity and flirtation, while both parties know that this public (and therefore visibly harmless) flirtation is a cover for the Duchess's real desire for

Dorian. This use of a sophisticated **subtext** to conceal sexual longing is an important linguistic skill in a world where the point of marriage is not love but the preservation of the ruling class. As Lord Henry says, 'Women are not always allowed a choice' (p. 157).

Wilde places much of the **social comedy** of the novel towards the end, when Dorian grows ever more afraid. The effect is to link these lively aristocrats, with all their sparkle, to our sense that a tragic end cannot be long deferred. Time is in many ways running out for all these witty speakers. Widening suffrage, the emancipation of women and the rise of the United States as a world power are not just subjects for their wit but forces that will change their lives.

Along with all the high wit, learned **allusions** and extensive vocabulary, Wilde also employs an effect that depends on none of these things. Neil Bartlett has pointed out that certain unremarkable words recur again and again: 'strange', 'languid', 'marvellous', 'brilliant' (*The Uses of Monotony*, 1994). Because they *do* recur, they become remarkable, as a monotonous beat is remarkable. Bartlett likens it to the act of tickling a trout, a prolonged caress that finally causes the fish to stop struggling and let the fisherman kill it.

While Lord Henry can hypnotise Dorian with his words, Wilde is also, from the outset, creating his own hypnotic rhythm that will only stop with the death of Dorian. This is underlined by the text's use of music. At every significant moment – meeting Lord Henry, going to the opera after the death of Sibyl, recalling the relationship with Alan Campbell that makes it possible to demand his help in destroying a corpse – Dorian is linked to music. Often the detail is very specific. The innocent Dorian is linked to the sweetness of Schumann; he is enticed away from grieving for Sibyl by the distinctive voice of a popular soprano; he plays a Chopin nocturne which is a farewell to Lord Henry. Many of Wilde's readers would know these pieces well enough to 'hear' a kind of soundtrack to the action. Dorian is both the player and the listener, hypnotised by music and using it to hypnotise the reader into following his extraordinary life.

**CONTEXT**

Robert Schumann (1810–56) is used here to evoke not only the pastoral sweetness of his *Forest Scenes* (1848–9) but also his image as a romantic lover. He waited many years for his pianist lover, Clara, whose father forbade her to marry, and he finally eloped with her.

 **QUESTION**

If you were asked to make a modern soundtrack for a film of the novel, what music would you pick for some of the key moments, and why?

## PART FOUR

## CRITICAL PERSPECTIVES

**CHECK THE BOOK**

Graham Hough's *The Last Romantics* (1949) is not at all favourable to Wilde. However, the innovative epilogue, an imaginary conversation between the poet W. B. Yeats and the novelist and historian H. G. Wells, set in Limbo, might have pleased Wilde with its use of the **dialogic form**, which he pioneered in his own essays such as *The Decay of Lying* (an imaginary debate in which the participants are named Cyril and Vivian, after Wilde's own sons).

## READING CRITICALLY

This section provides a range of critical viewpoints and perspectives on *The Picture of Dorian Gray* and gives a broad overview of key debates, interpretations and theories proposed since the novel was published. It is important to bear in mind the variety of interpretations and responses this text has produced, many of them shaped by the critics' own backgrounds and historical contexts.

No single view of the text should be seen as dominant – it is important that you arrive at your own judgements by questioning the perspectives described, and by developing your own critical insights. Objective analysis is a skill achieved through coupling close reading with an informed understanding of the key ideas, related texts and background information relevant to the text. These elements are all crucial in enabling you to assess the interpretations of other readers, and even to view works of criticism as texts in themselves. The ability to read critically will serve you well both in your study of *The Picture of Dorian Gray*, and in any critical writing, presentation, or further work you undertake.

## EARLY CRITICAL VIEWS

The most heated arguments over the *Lippincott's* version of *Dorian Gray* took place in three periodicals. The *St James's Gazette* review, of 20 June 1890, although published anonymously, was by Samuel Lord Henry Jeyes (1857–1932), an opponent of *The Yellow Book* and its contributors (see **Literary background: The English Aesthetics**). Throughout, it briskly lambasted the characters as 'puppies' and the subject-matter as 'disgusting', and attributed two possible motives to Wilde: a desire to shock the public with hints about homosexuality, or such hunger for fame that he would settle for attracting the same kind of notice as a bad smell. Jeyes talked airily of censorship, though he did not call for the banning of the book. Much of his hostility was grounded in class prejudice: commenting that one should not expect such a 'stupid and vulgar' book from a man who, educated at Oxford, had had 'the opportunity of associating with gentlemen' (quoted in Karl Beckson, *Oscar Wilde: The Critical Heritage*, 1970, p. 69), he went on to attack the social sweep of the novel by linking it to another and very dissimilar piece of work, W. T. Stead's crusading article on child prostitution, *The Maiden Tribute of Modern Babylon*. Jeyes described Wilde and Stead as 'simpleton poseurs (whether they call themselves Puritan or Pagan) who know nothing about the life which they affect to have explored' (*St James's Gazette*, 20 June 1890; Beckson, p. 67). The *Scots Observer* also indulged in sexual and class bias by mockingly alluding to the Cleveland Street Scandal, remarking, 'if he can write for none but outlawed noblemen and perverted telegraph-boys, the sooner he takes to tailoring (or some other decent trade) the better for his own reputation and the public morals' (*Scots Observer*, 8 July 1890). The *Daily Chronicle* produced an ornate and wordy passage about 'the mephitic odours of moral and spiritual putrefaction' in the book (Hart-Davis, p. 85).

Wilde wrote vigorously in his own defence to these three alone 'out of the two hundred and sixteen criticisms that have passed from my library table to the waste-paper basket' (quoted in Hart-Davis, p. 85). He called for freedom of expression and defended the 'ethical beauty' of his work, pointing out repeatedly the difference between a writer and the characters he creates – although his trial was to make it painfully clear that numerous readers, including the prosecution, remained incapable of grasping this point. Reviews of the revised 1891 edition were more muted, but none really came to terms with the idea that fantasy and mannered comedy could engage with serious issues as effectively as naturalism. 'Brilliant', sniffed *Theatre* magazine, 'as a sick man's eye' (quoted in Beckson, p. 81).

## LATER CRITICISM

Criticism during the years after the Second World War was powerfully shaped by the thought of F. R. Leavis (1895–1978) and in particular his book *The Great Tradition* (1948), which located the value of the English novel in its 'moral seriousness' and fine-tuned

**CHECK THE BOOK**

Karl Beckson's *Oscar Wilde: The Critical Heritage* (1970) is a compendium of critical responses to Wilde's work from 1881 onwards. It usefully charts the way that different eras have responded to the man and how this has affected judgements on his work.

naturalistic rendition of a socially diverse and complex world of human relations. This was not especially favourable to the stylised playfulness of Wilde. Graham Hough's *The Last Romantics* (1949), examining the failure of English writers of the *fin de siècle* (see **Historical background: Wealth and dissidence**) to achieve 'accommodation between art and a bourgeois industrial society' (p. xix), labels Wilde as derivative of Baudelaire and Huysmans (see **Literary background: Decadents and Symbolists**) and accuses him of importing inappropriate 'social smartness' into the 'emotional and sensual intensity at which [he] is aiming in *Dorian Gray*' (Hough, p. 200). It was some time before Wilde's non-naturalistic forms could be understood as innovative tools for moral critique, and not an evasion of it. Prejudice against his sexuality (which Hough coyly mentions in French, as if English lacked an appropriate term) was at least partly responsible.

Christopher Nassaar's *Into the Demon Universe* (1974) was one of the first post-war books to take Wilde seriously. It offers an interpretation of *Dorian Gray* as an **allegory** about art, suggesting that Basil represents the Pre-Raphaelite movement (see **Themes: Art**), which 'recognise[s] the evil within the self and deals seriously with it … in small doses' (Nassaar, p. 66), only to be destroyed by the more energetic Decadent movement, just as Basil is destroyed by Dorian. However, Nassaar's image of Wilde creating a 'religion of evil' (Nassaar, p. xvi) ignores the variety and complexity of his work. It assumes Wilde equated his own homosexuality with the demonic, a reading that considers only the guilt Wilde felt towards his family and ignores the generous and cheerful aspects of his relationships. It also takes no account of the novel's clear distinction between the love of Basil and that of Lord Henry.

## THE LAST TWENTY YEARS

More recently, Wilde scholarship has paid tribute to the originality of his thought and the breadth of his talent. Wilde's treatment of female experience has been widely reappraised, and his understanding of the plight of the educated woman in a world of double standards and social and sexual change has led to new

---

**CONTEXT**

Nassaar's view is anticipated by a *Punch* cartoon (19 July 1890) in which Wilde is shown as 'The Fad Boy' (that is, 'fat' said with an Irish accent), forcing a copy of *Dorian Gray* on a prudish 'Mrs Grundy'. In Dickens's *Pickwick Papers*, the Fat Boy likes to tell stories, which he introduces with 'I wants to make your flesh creep'.

---

readings of his plays. In a highly original approach to Wilde concentrating on his relationship with his public, Regenia Gagnier suggests that *Dorian Gray* is focused towards a female readership. She also suggests that Sibyl Vane, brilliant in her ability to adopt roles (and a victim of masculine egotism), is more truly representative of Wilde than any of the male characters in the novel (Gagnier, ch. 6).

Post-Colonial scholarship has paid particular attention to Wilde the Irishman. Declan Kiberd's *Inventing Ireland* (1995) presents him as a 'militant republican'. In *Heathcliff and the Great Hunger*, Terry Eagleton explores the evolution of Wilde's thought, from an early identification with social Darwinism in a student essay of 1879 to a complex understanding of the nature of self and society, springing from his place in a crumbling Anglo-Irish Ascendancy increasingly unsure of its identity. He suggests that as 'socialite and sodomite, republican and dandy' (Eagleton, p. 331) Wilde experienced tension between the idea of the self as the product of natural laws and the idea of the self created through its choices (see **Reading *The Picture of Dorian Gray***), which he could explore fully only in fiction. As Eagleton points out, Wilde's choice of literary form was political: ancient Irish traditions of story-telling were not realistic, and while Irish writers understood Victorian naturalism, many ignored it – in favour of the Gothic tradition Wilde modernises in *Dorian Gray*, or a stylised treatment of the English language (which, like Wilde, they spoke with an alien accent), tipping into extravagant **social comedy** on the edge of parody.

**CHECK THE BOOK**

Terry Eagleton discusses fellow Irishmen Bram Stoker and Oscar Wilde in 'Running out of Soil', a review of a biography of Stoker for the *London Review of Books*, 2 December 2004. You can find a detailed account of Wilde's political development in Eagelton's *Heathcliff and the Great Hunger* (1995).

It is a mark of Wilde's achievement in creating his own personality that research on his life is continually updated and revised. Even the detailed and scrupulous work of Richard Ellmann's biography has been modified and corrected: for example, in Neil McKenna's *The Secret Life of Oscar Wilde* (2003) and in Thomas Wright's *Oscar's Books* (2008), an original biography which tracks Wilde's life and ideas through the books that he owned (many of which fed into *Dorian Gray*). Neil Bartlett's *Who Was That Man? A Present for Mr Oscar Wilde* (1988) entwines a meditation on Wilde's experience with Bartlett's own as a gay man in the London of the 1980s. Writing in a spirit of affection ('We're walking your streets,' he writes to Wilde, p. 212), Bartlett also reproaches Wilde for his evasiveness in the dock at a point when society was establishing a definition of 'homosexuality': 'He lied, and he lied at a crucial moment in our history, just when we were about to appear' (p. 33).

Terry Eagleton's 1989 play *Saint Oscar* explores Wilde's relationship with Irish nationalism and with Speranza (see **Oscar Wilde's life and works**). David Hare's 1998 play *The Judas Kiss* shows his relationship with Bosie both before and after the trial. In 1998 the painter and sculptor Maggi Hambling created a statue incorporating a seat of green granite. Entitled *A Conversation with Oscar Wilde*, it shows him smoking a cigarette. Since it was placed in Adelaide Street near Trafalgar Square, the cigarette has been stolen on many occasions, but people continue to sit there and the 'conversation' goes on.

## CONTEMPORARY APPROACHES

### MARXIST CRITICISM

**CHECK THE NET**

Maggi Hambling's statue was nominated as an 'icon of England' in an online exploration of material relating to England's cultural heritage. You can see an image of the statue by going to **http://www.icons. org.uk** and typing 'Oscar Wilde' into the Search box.

Marxist critics attempt to understand literature from the perspective of the 'historical materialism' developed by Marx and Engels: that is, as a form of material production which is part of the processes of history and the class struggle and which also illuminates them. They are concerned not only with the direct discussion of these subjects within a text, but also with what the text does *not* say. The **ideology** of a culture – shared beliefs and values held in an unquestioning manner – is like water to a fish, invisible and unacknowledged. Dominant groups in society have no need to articulate their exclusion of others. They perceive the status quo as an organic growth, rather than a structure allowing them to exercise power.

A Marxist critic might thus look at a text and ask, 'Whose story does this tell? Is it told at the expense of exploited groups?' *Dorian Gray* might read rather differently, for instance, if told from the point of view of Sibyl Vane. But if Wilde chooses a protagonist from the aristocracy, he forces us to ask some tough questions about the unspoken assumption of social power as Lord Henry exults 'I am so glad you have never done anything' (p. 172). Lord Henry has produced nothing but his protégé, Dorian, who in turn produces only his own life as a work of art. In short, their class produces only itself. To do so, it depends on the work of those who are productive. Dorian can turn himself into a work of dandified art because the product of Basil's labour, the painting, sustains his eternal youth and beauty (and inherited wealth gives him eternal leisure).

While Sibyl's story forms only a part of Dorian's, she is his exact working-class counterpart. For her, youth, beauty and talent are simultaneously assets she markets and qualities she must struggle to preserve in order to go on working. Dorian assumes both the authority of an aristocratic husband and the bourgeois power of a manager launching a star. When her talent disappears in the face of this double ownership, Sibyl ceases to exist for Dorian as a person. He perceives her first as a burden to assume out of sentimental guilt, and then as a literary construct with no material or economic existence. Nothing changes as a result of her death. The surface of the aristocratic world is unbroken by the destruction of those whose labour supports it. Even Basil disappears almost without a trace.

## PSYCHOANALYTIC CRITICISM

Literature has often found it useful to employ ideas and terminology from psychoanalysis, and vice versa. Psychoanalytic critics of *Dorian Gray* have found a fruitful crossover in the work of French psychiatrist Jacques Lacan (1901–81). In 1949 he began to explore 'the mirror stage' in human development. As he points out, a baby of around six months, still unable to stand independently and held tightly by an adult, will become entranced by his or her image in the mirror. The baby is still uncoordinated, its hands flailing aimlessly, and experiences its own body as fragmented and uncontrollable. In contrast, the image seems whole and in command of itself. To deal with its fear and rage at confronting a superior 'rival', the baby identifies with it, and remains trapped in fascination with the illusory image forever. Lacan describes the recognition of the self in the mirror as 'jubilation' – a sense of mastery – but as the baby realises how fragile its own mastery is compared to the power of the adult holding it up to the mirror, it is devastated. Throughout our lives, we continue to experience the baby's sense of loss and are haunted by the hopeless desire of the mirror stage.

**CHECK THE BOOK**

A recent and useful account of how Marxism can be applied (or not) to literary studies is Terry Eagleton's *Criticism and Ideology: A Study in Marxist Literary Theory* (2006).

**CONTEXT**

In Act I of his **social comedy** *A Woman of No Importance*, Wilde puts some acid comments about class relations into the mouth of a young American girl who proclaims that England 'lies like a leper in purple. It sits like a dead thing smeared with gold.' The line was cut after booing was heard at the London premiere. However, Wilde retained it in the published edition, and on the play's first night in New York it was applauded.

This process can be seen in Dorian's own relationship to his portrait, in front of which he flushes with pleasure as he 'recognise[s] himself for the first time' (p. 23). The picture is at once his rival, with the eternal youth he can never have and inspiring his murderous rage, and an object of desire that he refuses to give up to Lord Henry. Loving it and hating it, he can never let it go: it is himself. But he also believes, like the baby confused by the apparent wholeness of its image, that it has a power he does not have, and at times imagines that it is making demands on him to kill or to confess his sins.

Dorian also experiences a distorted version of what Lacan called entry into the Symbolic order. Lacan describes the roles of Father and Mother in initiating the child as a speaker of language (both terms are used symbolically, rather than to denote the actual biological parents). It is the Father who bears the true responsibility because he possesses the phallus while the mother does not; thus the Father makes the child aware of difference, the basis on which language is founded.

Dorian is an orphan. He knows his mother only through paintings, which show her in disguise – dressed as a Bacchante, for example – and without Dorian. He has, however, several men to fill the role of father: the elderly, cruel Kelso, the image of what he does not wish to be; the detached Lord Henry, who tells him to treat others like works of art, with no more capacity for feeling than images in a mirror; and Basil, who in a sense 'fathers' him more than once. Basil triggers a second 'birth' in Dorian by creating the painted image that allows his body to enjoy an eternal youth. Through murdering Basil (as Oedipus murdered his father) after eighteen years of changeless good looks, Dorian embarks on a third phase of life. Despite his name ('Basil' derives from the Greek for 'king') and his attempts to make Dorian do right, Basil cannot impose the law because he cannot impose difference. He has painted his love into the picture – Dorian's mirror – so completely that his own self cannot be disentangled from Dorian's. Lacking both mother and father (in the symbolic sense) Dorian is condemned to eternal desire, with no chance of true adulthood. He never fully enters into language by articulating new ideas, but simply parrots Lord Henry.

**CHECK THE NET**

You can find Lacan's influential (and difficult) paper 'The mirror stage as formative of the function of the I as revealed in psychoanalytic experience' (delivered at the 16th International Congress of Psychoanalysis, Zürich, 17 July 1949) with some helpful annotations at **http://courses.essex.ac.uk**. Click on Department of Literature, Film and Theatre Studies, then the course called 'Approaches to Text'. You can find Lacan in the Glossary.

And without the Law that a less blindly adoring Basil might have brought him, he retains all the selfish amorality of a baby.

Lacan claimed (in *Écrits: A Selection*, trans. Alan Sheridan, 1977, p. 1) that his writings were not meant to be intellectually understood, but that reflections upon them would produce a meaningful effect in the reader. Certainly his ideas have generated a large number of articles on *Dorian Gray* with a range of very different perspectives (see **Contemporary approaches: Queer theory**, below).

## QUEER THEORY

Queer theory assumes that it is meaningless to classify people on the basis of any shared characteristic and label them 'women', 'men' or 'homosexuals'. Rather than being fixed, identities comprise various aspects that we perform, including our gender. Judith Butler's seminal *Gender Trouble* (1990) suggests that gender is what you *do* at a particular time – mothering, being a husband, loving someone of the same sex – rather than a changeless truth about you. Certain gender configurations have come to seem natural in our culture, but they do not have to be.

Queer theory encourages people to choose the kind of performance they give in order to change our limited understanding of masculinity and femininity as polar opposites – something Dorian, for all his adventures, fails to do. He performs some conventional gender roles well, for example as discreet adulterer at the parties of the wealthy. However, his obsessive concealment of other sexual activities does not change attitudes, but confirms them as criminal or at least socially disastrous, and his devil's bargain precludes the possibility of performing the role of permanent partner by ensuring that he cannot age and die alongside a loved one. As the years go on, Dorian wearies of the choices left to him. He lacks real interest in house-party sexual games. The text's repeated description of him as a 'young man', complete with petulant and boyish gestures, during his last, fatal encounter with Basil underlines the incongruity between the flawless body and the acts it performs. Perhaps the only role of which Dorian does not tire is one specific to his class

**CHECK THE BOOK**

For examples using Lacan's ideas in relation to *Dorian Gray*, try Stephen Arata, *Fictions of Loss in the Victorian Fin de Siècle* (2009).

and era as well as his gender: that of Male Heir to a fortune which he can spend on the luxury and secrecy that supports all his chosen masks.

**CHECK THE BOOK**

Riki Wilchins's *Queer Theory, Gender Theory: An Instant Primer* (2004) is a useful introduction to queer theory.

Butler also suggests, in *Bodies that Matter* (1993), that while psychoanalytic theory has generally understood the processes of identification with someone (wanting to be like them) and desire for someone (wanting to possess them) as totally separate, this perception underpins a false logic of 'compulsory heterosexuality' by insisting that we cannot and must not desire those we might wish to imitate. Steven Bruhm's *Reflecting Narcissus* (2001) takes off from this standpoint to offer a useful Queer reading of Wilde's novel. It deconstructs the view of early psychologists that homosexual desire is, like Narcissus's longing to possess the person he sees reflected in the water, essentially a regression to an immature sexuality leading only to cruelty, sterility and death. Rather, it suggests that in *Dorian Gray* Wilde shows the role of Narcissus performed in a variety of ways that comment on one another.

Dorian destroys himself through self-love, but in Basil Hallward we have an alternative image of narcissistic desire as a creative force. The portrait is a reflection of Basil's own love for Dorian and also an invitation to Dorian to view that love shining from the painted image of his own face – one that he fails to interpret. While *Dorian Gray* remains a moral parable with a tragic end for its flawed hero, it also suggests that a more fruitful engagement with narcissistic desire is possible to artists of all kinds, of whom Basil is the representative. Not all need be subject to his fate.

## PART FIVE

## BACKGROUND

## OSCAR WILDE'S LIFE AND WORKS

'I was a man who stood in symbolic relations to the art and culture of my age' (quoted in Holland, p. 912).

Oscar Wilde's verdict on himself was not exaggerated. To a society on the edge of a new century he offered new styles of language, dress and manner and new possibilities for constructing one's personal identity. That society responded by making him into both celebrity and outsider, hero and victim.

Oscar Fingal O'Flahertie Wills Wilde (the first two names from Irish legend, the third from Irish nobility and the fourth from a noted Irish playwright) was born on 16 October 1854 in Dublin. Ireland was still recovering from the Great Famine. Wilde's father, a noted surgeon, wrote a report on its impact; his mother, radically politicised by it, wrote nationalist poetry and journalism under the name 'Speranza' (Italian for 'hope'). The flamboyant and eccentric couple were the centre of a noted literary and political circle. 'It is only tradespeople who are respectable,' Speranza announced; 'we are above respectability' (quoted in Richard Canning, *Oscar Wilde*, 2008, p. 10). However, Wilde and his brother Willie were sent to the orthodox and very English Portora Royal School, known as 'the Eton of Ireland'. Wilde disliked it, but achieved a Classical Scholarship to Trinity College, Dublin, where he was taught by noted scholar John Mahaffy and helped with the editing of his book *Social Life in Greece*. Increasingly drawn to England, Wilde won a 'Demyship' at Magdalen College, Oxford, in 1874.

Wilde considered his Oxford years a 'flower-like' time (Hart-Davis, p. 110). He attended lectures by John Ruskin, Slade Professor of Fine Art, the champion of medieval art and craft and the virtues of manual work, and even boasted of pushing 'Mr Ruskin's especial wheelbarrow' during an attempt to demonstrate the dignity of labour by building a road in neighbouring Ferry Hinksey. He was

### CONTEXT

Before the Married Women's Property Act of 1882, a husband had absolute rights over his wife's money. William Wilde had used up all Speranza's marriage settlement. She wrote scathingly of the way women were left with 'pin money … the husband reserving all the rest for himself and giving the wife no account of it' (quoted in John Sloan, *Authors in Context: Oscar Wilde*, 2003, p. 41).

**CONTEXT**

Wilde appears in William Powell Frith's 1881 painting *A Private View at the Royal Academy*. He can easily be picked out among the crowd by his commanding height, his buttonhole and his clean-shaven chin amid a forest of Victorian whiskers.

**CONTEXT**

The American-born James Abbot McNeill Whistler (1834–1903) was active mainly in England. His work owed much to the Symbolists and treated his subjects as arrangements in colour and tone rather than as images to be copied to the life. Whistler also created the famous Peacock Room for the London home of the Liverpool shipping magnate Frederick Leyland (now reconstructed in the Freer Gallery, Washington).

equally influenced by Walter Pater, who rejected medieval collectivism in favour of the art of the Renaissance with its celebration of individualism and the sensuous life, and considered Pater's *The Renaissance* his 'golden book' (quoted in Ellmann, p. 80) (see **Literary background: The English Aesthetics**). Like many student contemporaries, Wilde was attracted to the Roman Catholic Church, but in the end there were doctrines he could not accept and social disadvantages he preferred not to endure in an England riven with religious prejudice, though he loved Catholic ritual all his life.

The image Wilde projected at Oxford was that of an extrovert, idle dandy, famous for his reddish-brown coat modelled on a cello (he claimed the pattern came to him in a dream) and for filling his rooms with lilies. However, he read voraciously and travelled in Italy and Greece with Mahaffy. (This desire to visit the birthplace of classical literature puzzled the Oxford dons.) It was no surprise, to him at least, when he achieved a double first and won the Newdigate Prize for poetry in 1879.

However, the death of Wilde's father in 1876 had revealed that the family was seriously in debt. Wilde was painfully aware of the need to earn his living. The magazine trade was flourishing, and he moved to London hoping to market himself as an exponent of 'aesthetics'. He made contacts in the art world, including the painter James McNeill Whistler; he befriended noted actresses of the day, including Sarah Bernhardt and the most beloved figure on the English stage, Ellen Terry. His interest in the business of shaping and projecting a personality also made him a trusted advisor of the mistress of the Prince of Wales, Lily Langtry, as she began working on the stage.

Wilde published a volume of poetry at his own expense, which received mixed reviews but eventually ran through five editions. He wrote a tragedy, *Vera: Or, the Nihilists*, based on the story of a young Russian woman who shot the Chief of the St Petersburg police in 1878. This was tactfully declined by Ellen Terry, but Mrs Bernard Beere, who became a lifelong and loyal friend, liked the play and planned to star in a London production in December 1881.

Encouraged, Wilde began another play, *A Florentine Tragedy*, in the tradition of the 'strange lurid' Jacobean drama to which Lord Henry likens the death of Sibyl Vane (p. 82). But his theatrical career faced an unexpected setback: the assassination of Czar Alexander II in March. Government pressure was applied to ban *Vera* – the Prince of Wales was related to the Russian royal family – and rehearsals were called off.

However, he had a new opportunity. Wilde and his circle were sufficiently well known to generate cartoons and parodies, and in April 1881 Gilbert and Sullivan made a hit with their comic opera *Patience,* a skit on the aesthetic movement with a hero in green velvet who urges his followers to 'walk down Piccadilly with a poppy or a lily in your medieval hand'. They planned an American tour, but there was one difficulty: America might miss the jokes. So Wilde was paid to give lectures on aesthetics right across the USA. He sailed in January 1882, that month's *Punch* carrying a cartoon of a weeping maiden in Pre-Raphaelite drapery waving to the SS *Arizona.*

Wilde prepared for his tour carefully. He made use of the Gilbert and Sullivan stereotype when it suited him, but worked to establish himself as thinker and wit in his own right. When sixty Harvard students attended a lecture wearing velvet breeches and carrying sunflowers, Wilde arrived in dinner jacket and trousers. His lectures anticipated the lifestyle programmes popular on television today: practical advice mediated though an appealing personality. Campaigning against early Victorian décor, a glum and stuffy style designed to display the wealth of the householder, he tapped into a hunger for colour, light and modernity.

He crisscrossed America on a heavy schedule of lectures in venues from opera houses to mechanics' institutes. The press could be hostile but Wilde charmed some unlikely audiences: Leadville miners named a lode (a vein of silver ore) after him (although he lamented the lack of free shares). He met American authors, of whom perhaps the most significant to him was the radically innovative homosexual poet Walt Whitman. Wilde described Whitman as 'the spirit who lived blamelessly but dared to kiss the smitten mouth of his own century' (quoted in Ellmann, p. 164). By

**CONTEXT**

In 1882 *Punch* carried a cartoon of Wilde as 'Maudle', a plump and oily aesthete trying to convince a country bumpkin that her son does not need a profession: 'Why should he be anything? Why not let him remain forever content to EXIST BEAUTIFULLY?'

**CONTEXT**

Wilde wrote of the miners: 'They ... took me to a dancing saloon, where I saw the only rational method of art criticism I have ever come across. Over the piano was printed a notice: "Please do not shoot the pianist – he is doing his best." The mortality among pianists in that place is marvellous' (quoted in Sheridan Morley, *Oscar Wilde*, 1976, p. 44).

**CHECK THE BOOK**

The idea of criticism as an art form in itself is discussed in the chapter 'Literary Criticism and Literary Creation' in David Lodge's book *Consciousness and the Novel* (2002).

**CHECK THE BOOK**

Laurel Brake's *Subjugated Knowledges: Journalism, Gender and Literature 1837–1907* (1994) gives an account of Wilde's editorship of *Woman's World*. Among his innovations was a series of illustrations headlined 'The Woodland Gods' – young men modelling Orlando's costumes for an outdoor production of Shakespeare's *As You Like It*. Slender and elegant, they could serve as images of Dorian, or indeed Sibyl in her Ganymede costume described in Chapter 6.

the time of his return Wilde had earned $11,000 and secured a New York production for *Vera*.

He immediately set off for Paris, where he encountered the Symbolists (also known as the Decadents), who united a style grounded in extreme emotional states with anarchist politics. They offered Wilde a more theoretically developed understanding of culture than the English tradition, and he was soon to expound his political theories in essays as well as fiction, taking the Symbolist view that criticism was itself an art form. Typically, he also changed his look, cutting his hair and adopting the black overcoat and silk hat favoured by Parisian men.

Wilde had now garnered enough material to tour England, 'civilising the provinces' as he called it, with lectures on 'Experiences in America' and 'The House Beautiful'. He could also afford to marry. His bride, Constance Lloyd, granddaughter of a rich QC, shared his enthusiasm for the Suffragette Movement and was a member of the Rational Dress Society, rejecting corsets for free-flowing gowns or even trousers. They had two sons, Cyril in 1885 and Vyvyan in 1886. Their house in Tite Street, decorated in modern style (some of the décor features in *Dorian Gray*), was the centre of a wide circle of writers, artists and critics.

In 1887 Wilde acquired a steady job editing the magazine *The Lady's World*; he changed the title to *Woman's World*, dropped the society gossip column and commissioned articles from women on female emancipation, women's colleges and Shakespeare.

From 1887 he began to concentrate on a literary career, although some of his work was slow to find a publisher. A short story, 'The Remarkable Rocket', explored art and vanity. A longer work, begun in 1887 but not published until 1889, *The Portrait of Mr W. H.*, is a 'tale within a tale' about a forged account of Shakespeare's romance with a boy player, Willie Hughes. This tale has a profound effect on both teller and listeners, one of whom disguises his death from consumption as suicide to convince others of his commitment to the story's truth. The narrator suggests 'men die for what they *want* to be true, for what some terror in their hearts tells them is not true' (Holland, p. 1201).

The frankness with which the early drafts of *The Portrait of Mr W. H.* dealt with homosexual desire reflected a shift in Wilde's own understanding of himself. In 1886 he had met seventeen-year-old 'Puck-faced' Robert Ross at Oxford, his first male lover and a lifelong friend. The relationship seemed to release a burst of creative energy.

Wilde explored some other themes of *Dorian Gray* in comic vein. *Lord Arthur Savile's Crime* ponders free will. When Podgers, a palmist, predicts that the hero will commit murder, he decides to get it over before his wedding day. He fails to despatch elderly relations with poison and an exploding clock, and then has a 'brilliant idea' (p. 190): he kills Podgers, and lives happily ever after. *The Canterville Ghost* mocks the conventions of Gothic horror as an American family prove too insensitive to be driven away by the ghost of the murdering aristocrat haunting their mansion. He steals watercolours to fake bloodstains, only to find them eradicated by the latest carpet cleaner. Wilde's first published success was a volume of fairy tales for children, *The Happy Prince and Other Stories,* based on stories he told Cyril and Vyvyan and drawing on the Irish folk stories he learned from his parents. A darker set of tales, *A House of Pomegranates,* followed in 1891.

While touring Philadelphia Wilde had met publisher John Marshall Stoddart, who came to England seven years later as agent for *Lippincott's Monthly Magazine.* Over lunch with Wilde and Arthur Conan Doyle, Stoddart commissioned short novels. Doyle's was the second Sherlock Holmes novel, *The Sign of Four.* Stoddart found Wilde's first attempt, 'The Fisherman and His Soul', too short (see **Themes: The Double**). Wilde worked at speed to produce an alternative, the first version of *The Picture of Dorian Gray.* That he could do so in a few months reflects his need for cash (£200 for the serial rights), but it was also a chance for him to draw together strands of his critical and political thinking and celebrate his infatuation with a young poet, John Gray.

When *Dorian Gray* appeared in July 1890 in the US edition of *Lippincott's,* it sold out. The British press, however, was uniformly disapproving and copies were withdrawn from the newsstands.

**CONTEXT**

'The Remarkable Rocket' is a sly dig at Whistler. In 1877 Ruskin denounced Whistler's *Nocturne in Black and Gold: The Falling Rocket,* accusing him of 'flinging a pot of paint in the public's face'. Whistler sued for libel the following year. He won, but was awarded only a farthing damages.

 **CHECK THE NET**

You can see *The Falling Rocket* and other works by Whistler at **http://www.ibiblio. org** – search for Whistler.

**CONTEXT**

A week before his court appearance, Wilde himself visited a palmist, Mrs Robinson, who told him that the trial would be a success. It is impossible to know whether this affected his decision not to leave England, especially given the flippant tone of *Lord Arthur Savile's Crime*. Neil Bartlett's play *In Extremis* (2000) imagines the encounter between Wilde and the fortune-teller. It premiered at the National Theatre on 3 November 2000, with Corin Redgrave as Wilde and Sheila Hancock as Mrs Robinson.

Wilde's new book-length version was accepted by his second choice of publisher. Longer, less explicit and more reflective, it was composed while Wilde worked simultaneously on 'The Soul of Man Under Socialism', inspired by a speech of Bernard Shaw's. The assertion in 'The Soul of Man' that everyone, not just the wealthy or the guardians of orthodox morality, has a right and a duty to become an individual – 'he who would lead a Christ-like life is he who is perfectly and absolutely himself' (Holland, p. 1181) – provides a possible gloss on the story of Dorian.

Disappointed in his *Dorian Gray* royalties, Wilde turned to the stage as a likelier source of income and began a series of **social comedies** which dominated the West End between 1892 and 1895. Widely perceived as the best of their kind since Sheridan's, they deal, like *Dorian Gray*, with hypocrisy, but the secrets are social rather than supernatural: sexual indiscretion and political sleaze. *Lady Windermere's Fan*, staged in 1892, showed a 'fallen' woman meeting the puritanical daughter who believes her to be dead, and saving her from the mistakes she made herself. The following year *A Woman of No Importance* set a witty aristocratic circle like that in *Dorian Gray* (even recycling some of the jokes) against a group of earnest puritans: an unmarried mother riven with guilt, her stolid son and the young American heiress who loves him. *An Ideal Husband*, two years later, showed a politician blackmailed for insider dealing being rescued by an apparently frivolous, witty idler. It opened to great acclaim at the Haymarket and was still playing when Wilde's greatest comedy, *The Importance of Being Earnest*, premiered a month later on Valentine's Day. This 'trivial comedy for serious people' made fun of all social conflicts – between the sexes, between the classes, between manners and desire – and resolved them in a farce about two young men who pretend to be brothers and then find out that they are, in a joyous parody of the sinister doubling in *Dorian Gray*.

By now Wilde himself had a double life. Shortly after the publication of *Dorian Gray* he fell in love with Lord Alfred 'Bosie' Douglas, younger son of the Marquess of Queensberry. Unstable, manipulative and capricious, Bosie made it difficult for Wilde to concentrate on work even while his extravagance made the work necessary. He even demanded the right to do the French translation of Wilde's play *Salome* (as a biblical story, it was banned in England), a task for which he was quite unqualified.

Both Wilde and Bosie had affairs with other men – inevitably risky, but Bosie's carelessness was disastrous. Wilde was blackmailed after Bosie gave a lover a cast-off suit with a letter from Wilde in the pocket. Wilde resolved this situation with humour and grace, but the real dangers lay in Bosie's explosive relationship with his brutal father. Queensberry threatened to shoot Bosie if he continued his 'loathsome' relationship with Wilde: Bosie responded by carrying a pistol, which to Wilde's embarrassment he discharged in the Berkeley hotel. Wilde tried to break with him, but tragedy intervened. Queensberry's first son, Viscount Drumlanrig, committed suicide in October 1894: his name was linked to the Foreign Secretary, Lord Rosebery, but the affair was hushed up as Rosebery took over the ailing Liberal government. Maddened by grief, Queensberry made a scapegoat of Wilde. He sent an insulting card to Wilde's club – as well as being misspelt, it was almost indecipherable.

Wilde was ambivalent about suing for libel, but Bosie was fiercely determined to put his father in the dock. Queensberry pleaded justification, his detectives locating several former lovers of Wilde so that Bosie did not have to appear in court. A warrant was issued for Wilde's arrest. Most in his position fled to Europe but Wilde refused, though Robbie Ross and Constance tried to persuade him. He declared: 'I shall stay and do my sentence, whatever it is' (quoted in Ellmann, p. 429). Given that his relationships would have been legal only a few years previously, he may have hoped it would be light. However, Queensberry's counsel (Wilde's onetime friend Edward Carson, who went on to orchestrate the partition of Ireland) graphically presented homosexuality as a serious threat to the class system. When he implied that Wilde had got two young working-class men drunk on champagne, Wilde replied 'What gentleman would stint his friends?' 'What gentleman,' sneered Carson, 'would stint the valet and the groom?' (quoted in Hyde, p. 144). Wilde drew applause when asked to explain a poem by Bosie ending 'I am the Love that dare not speak its name'. Drawing

**CHECK THE FILM**

Oscar Wilde's flamboyant personality and troubled life have given rise to a number of novels, plays and films. Brian Gilbert's 1998 film *Wilde*, starring Stephen Fry, is the most recent film about his life.

CONTEXT

One of Wilde's first substantial pieces of writing after his release was a letter to the *Daily Chronicle* about the regime in gaol and its potentially brutalising effect on the prisoners. It included a demand for the reinstatement of Warder Martin, who had been kind to Wilde and who had been dismissed for giving a biscuit to a child prisoner in distress.

CONTEXT

A statue of Wilde by Danny Osborne (b. 1949) was unveiled in Merrion Square, Dublin, on 28 October 1997. It shows a surprisingly slender Wilde sprawled at ease with a pipe and a book, wearing a colourful smoking jacket.

on the text of *Dorian Gray*, Wilde replied, 'There is nothing unnatural about it. It is intellectual, and it repeatedly exists between an elder and a younger man, when the elder man has intellect, and the younger man has all the joy, hope and glamour of life before him' (quoted in Hyde, p. 236). The first trial was inconclusive. The second brought a verdict of guilty, and Wilde received the maximum sentence: two years in prison with hard labour.

Gaol – Pentonville, then Reading – was harsh. Like his fellow prisoners, Wilde suffered from hunger, insomnia and dysentery. He heard a mentally disturbed man screaming as he was flogged. He emerged briefly to be declared bankrupt, theatre managers flocking to buy the rights to his work at bargain rates. Speranza died, and Constance, herself ill, came to Reading to break the news. He never saw her or his children again. He wrote a fifty-thousand-word letter to Douglas, *De Profundis*, a mixture of prison diary, reproach and political ideas, though the full text was not published until they were both dead.

On his release Wilde sailed to Dieppe, where he was met by Robbie Ross, and settled in Berneval. He composed his best poem, *The Ballad of Reading Gaol*, the story of a fellow prisoner hanged for murder, which was published under the name C.3.3, Wilde's prison number. He lived briefly with Bosie in Naples, painfully aware that they no longer loved each other. He wandered Europe, in failing health and dependent on his friends for money. (Bosie, who inherited Queenberry's fortune, gave nothing.) By autumn 1900 Wilde was in Paris, bedridden. In mid-November he was diagnosed with cerebral meningitis. As he drifted in and out of consciousness, Robbie Ross brought a priest who admitted him into the Catholic Church and administered the last rites. He was buried at Bagneux, and then moved to Père Lachaise in 1909 to lie among the French literary elite. A window in his memory was consecrated in Westminster Abbey on Valentine's Day 1995, a century after the opening night of *The Importance of Being Earnest*. Taking part in the service were Wilde's grandson, Merlin Holland, and Alice Douglas, great-niece of Bosie.

# HISTORICAL BACKGROUND

## WEALTH AND DISSIDENCE

An unremarkable **comedy** performed in Paris in 1888 gave Wilde's era a name for itself: *fin de siècle*. Meaning 'the end of the century', this name invited nations and individuals to consider who they were and where they were going. For the British Empire, the mid-century had been a period of stability, symbolised by the Great Exhibition in 1851. Featuring items from all over the world, it showed Britain as 'the workshop of the world', producing a third of all manufactured goods.

However, changes were coming. Germany and the USA emerged as powerful rivals. Bad harvests precipitated an agricultural slump. The landed aristocracy maintained a precarious dominance, and many shared the determination of Lord Henry's brother to marry a rich American as new industrialists joined the ruling class. Meanwhile, the rural poor streamed into the cities, but few found work with a living wage. The words 'unemployment' and 'slum' were coined. The gap between rich and poor widened; though more people had the vote, it was not enough to halt political unrest and even fear of revolution. Victoria's Golden Jubilee year, 1887, saw 'Bloody Sunday', a massed protest in Trafalgar Square that was violently dispersed by police.

There were uncomfortable legacies of colonialism. In Ireland the slump led to evictions (resistance being illegal under the Irish Crimes Act), resulting in boycotts and violence. The Irish Nationalist trusted to smooth the progress to Home Rule, Charles Stewart Parnell, was ruined by sexual scandal. Wilde's essay 'The Soul of Man Under Socialism' expresses rage at journalists who 'nailed their own ears to the keyhole' (Holland, p. 1095) to destroy talented men like Parnell by violating their privacy. The Liberal Party split over Home Rule and, weakened, was unable to deliver its promised social reforms.

Another ugly legacy was that of the Opium Wars. Twice before 1860 the government, unwilling to pay in silver for Britain's massive

**CHECK THE BOOK**

You can read a full account of the two Opium Wars (1839–42 and 1856–60), which culminated in the destruction of the Emperor's Summer Palace, in *The Opium Wars: The Addiction of One Empire and the Corruption of Another* by W. Travis Haynes III and Frank Sanello (2003).

tea imports, went to war to force the Chinese to import opium: 'not a curse, but a comfort and benefit to the hard-working Chinese', according to the British firm who profited most (Hanes and Sanello, p. 1). Chinese workers in London gathered to smoke opium, but there were only a handful of 'opium houses' and few resembled the squalid dens described in *Dorian Gray*. However, intolerance towards non-medicinal use of the drug grew. Society feared the possibility of an addicted Britain: 'the judgement of God for our national iniquity towards China', as Gladstone put it (quoted in Hanes and Sanello, p. 1).

## NEW SCIENCES

It was an age of inventions that changed the world: the telephone, the wireless telegraph, cinematography and electric light. Other scientific discoveries prompted questions about what it meant to be human, notably Darwin's *Origin of Species* in 1859. In his 1891 essay 'The Critic As Artist', Wilde considered Darwinism alongside the emerging trends in biblical scholarship, which placed texts in their context rather than assuming them to be literal historical records. He concluded: 'The nineteenth century is a turning point in history, simply on account of the work of two men, Darwin and Renan, the one the critic of the Book of Nature, the other the critic of the Books of God' (Holland, p. 1058).

Some Victorians understood evolutionary theory as grounds for optimism about humanity's inevitable upward progress. Some used it as a reason not to help the weaker members of society: Lord Henry's strictures on philanthropy in Chapter 2 suggest that he is a social Darwinist. Others were frightened by the possibility that if humanity could evolve from ape-like forebears it could also regress. Public anxiety about the horrific Jack the Ripper murders of 1888 is encapsulated in a *Punch* cartoon called 'The Nemesis of Neglect'. Suggesting that the killings arose from social conditions in East London, it shows an ape-like killer, 'red-handed, furtive, ruthless, unerect': that is, sliding back down the evolutionary scale into beasthood. In 1892 Max Nordau's *Degeneration* expounded this possibility of reverse evolution at length, finding causes and symptoms of decline in increasing industrialisation and in the work of modern artists including Wagner, Ibsen and Wilde himself. When

**CONTEXT**

In the 1860s the scholar Ernest Renan (1823–92) was the first to attempt a biography of Jesus, claiming that the Bible was as subject as any book to historical investigation. His work enraged the Roman Catholic church, but *The Life of Jesus* was an immediate success and in six months the French edition sold 60,000 copies. Its popularity was due to Renan's beautiful prose, much admired by Wilde, and to its luminously humane image of Jesus the man.

the English translation appeared in 1895, the word 'degeneration' was already well established in the English vocabulary. By 1898 *The National Review* even applied it to English cricket (Dryden, p. 8) and the word was often used merely to indicate a form of behaviour, or a social class, of which the speaker disapproved.

The new science of criminology was rooted in the same assumptions. Its architects, Cesare Lombroso and his daughters Gina and Paola, proposed the existence of a 'criminal type', suggesting that criminals inherited mental disorders that made them, like children, unable to repress their violent instincts. The Lombrosos said criminals could be identified by their physical resemblance to 'primitive races', who embodied the 'childhood' of the human species.

## SEXUALITY AND THE PSYCHE

Psychiatry, too, was seeking to explain the human personality and was already hinting at the existence of motives and desires of which the individual might be unaware. Freud was experimenting with hypnosis and suggested that some bodily ailments originated in unacknowledged strains and repressed desires rather than physical causes. However, it was not until 1900 that he expounded in detail his theory of 'the unconscious'.

In 1891 William James described a number of real-life cases of 'alternating personality', suggesting that the human mind was as capable of fragmentation as that of Dr Jekyll (see **Literary background: The Victorian Gothic**). Campaigns for what Queen Victoria called 'women's rights and all its attendant horrors' (Sloan, p. 41) were growing ever more urgent, and changes were inevitable in education, the professions and the law as a result. Inevitably, this meant that psychiatry would focus on sexuality and sexual difference.

In 1886 Richard von Krafft-Ebing (1840–1902) published *Psychopathia Sexualis*, a scientific classification of 'sexual aberrations' (partly in Latin to underline the serious and non-pornographic nature of the work). He provided a vocabulary in which to discuss the relationship between sexuality and violence,

 **CHECK THE NET**

For the full text of Nordau's *Degeneration* in English, go to **http://www.archive.org/details/texts** and type 'Degeneration' into the search box.

coining the terms 'sadism' and 'masochism' and suggesting that sexual desire could be as powerful a motive for cruelty or murder as revenge or greed. He also brought into common currency a word coined by Swiss doctor Karoly Benkert in 1869, 'homosexual', which he juxtaposed with the term 'heterosexual'. Krafft-Ebing considered 'homosexuals' to be not criminal but victims of heredity or upbringing, with no choice – as opposed to what he called 'the perverse', who deliberately acted against their natures for sexual thrills or money. But he had ensured that what was previously seen as a sexual practice was now perceived as a pathological state and a kind of identity in itself.

## CRIME AND PUNISHMENT

The links between crime and sexuality gave rise to a variety of new legislation, some of it counter-productive. Syphilis was becoming a serious problem and the government's first solution was the Contagious Diseases Act of 1861, empowering the police to force suspected prostitutes to be examined for signs of disease. Given that walking alone in the street was considered viable grounds for suspicion, outraged women campaigned furiously for the Act's repeal and demanded greater male accountability. One of most prominent champion of prostitutes, Josephine Butler, quoted one of the women in her care: 'It is men, only men, from first to last that we have to do with ... . I was flung about from man to man ... we never get out of the hands of men till we die' (quoted in Walkowitz, p. 92).

An important part of Butler's platform was the raising of the age of consent from thirteen. Parliament stalled the issue for years, but in 1885 W. T. Stead of the *Pall Mall Gazette* published a four-part article called *The Maiden Tribute of Modern Babylon*, detailing the trafficking of women on a vast scale and describing how Stead had been able to 'buy' a young girl for five pounds. Couched in sensationalistic terms, the articles whipped up massive public indignation. Though disgraceful views were expressed in Parliamentary debates (some MPs remarked that the girls had already been defiled so it didn't matter what happened to them), the government had no choice but to act and the Criminal Law Amendment Act was swiftly passed.

**CHECK THE BOOK**

Lombroso's *Criminal Man* and its companion volume, Lombroso and Ferrera's *The Female Offender*, were published in English by Fisher Unwin in 1895. Profusely illustrated with pictures of 'criminal types', they were used by police forces across the world for almost a century.

The speed of the Amendment led to some poorly phrased measures which had problematic consequences. Regulations about what constituted a 'brothel' meant that many prostitutes were forced to work the streets, making them vulnerable to attack. Clause II, introduced by the Liberal Lord Henry Labouchère in an attempt to protect young boys as well as girls, criminalised even consenting homosexual acts between adults in private. Clause II meant that any man could now be accused of a 'crime' to which the only witness was his partner. The Cleveland Street scandal of 1889, when a member of the royal family escaped prosecution after a police raid on a brothel staffed by young Post Office workers (who did *not* escape prosecution), created a climate of prejudice that rendered homosexual men very vulnerable.

Rapidly, the Labouchère Amendment became known as 'the blackmailer's charter'. The practised way in which Dorian produces a letter written in advance in order to force Alan Campbell to get rid of Basil's body suggests that he is all too familiar with the mechanics of this process. Wilde had been blackmailed by men of lower social standing, and had handled the situation so that nobody had been disgraced. However, the Cleveland Street affair had created the desire for a high-profile prosecution. Arguably, some of those who might have saved Wilde were willing that he should be sacrificed so that figures in the government and the royal family might be spared. As many gay critics have since pointed out, Wilde's celebrity and the fact that he was one of the first to be prosecuted meant that the newly coined term 'homosexual' was irretrievably coloured by the image of Wilde, even though he had never applied it to himself.

The prisons to which Victorian convicts were sent were also changing. The emphasis of the Victorian penal code was on repentance, reform and hard work. In practice this could be worse than the punishments of the previous century designed to terrify the onlooker into obedience. Prisoners were forbidden to speak to one another, as they were supposed to concentrate on their sins. They were denied reading matter other than religious tracts. They worked at 'picking oakum' – the recycling of old tarry rope – which caused agonising pain in the hands or spent long hours walking on the

**CHECK THE BOOK**

In 1895 H. G. Wells's *The Time Machine* launched his career as a novelist. In this early science fiction story, a traveller journeys into a future apparently ruled by the vacuous and charming Eloi, who delegate tasks to a subterranean workforce, the Morlocks. Later the traveller learns that the Morlocks control society and the Eloi are the remnants of a degenerate aristocracy kept for meat. He reflects, 'Man had been content to live in ease and delight upon the labours of his fellow man … and in the fullness of time Necessity had come home to him' (p. 56).

CRIME AND PUNISHMENT continued

treadmill, the whole point of which was that it achieved nothing. Flogging was the standard means of maintaining discipline.

Prisoners were also subjected to endless sermons and Bible readings. Wilde noted that the uniformly most hated aspect of prison life was this charade of Christian benevolence. It seemed that his fellow prisoners shared his opinion of Victorian hypocrisy and might well have found Lord Henry's loathing of 'philanthropy' very much to their taste.

## LITERARY BACKGROUND

### REALISM VERSUS ROMANCE

Wilde was working in a period of debate about the style and function of the novel, and in particular its relationship to **realism**. The novels of the mid-century had begun to explore in depth the relationship between people and their social, political and material circumstances, whether they were concerned with wars across whole continents like Tolstoy's *War and Peace* (1865–9) or the discontents of small-town bourgeois marriage like Flaubert's *Madame Bovary* (1857).

English novels of the period tended to tie the endings up neatly with marriages, legacies and coincidence (virtually every character in Dickens is appropriately rewarded or punished), but as the century wore on the influence of novelist, playwright and critic Émile Zola (1840–1902) became apparent. In his manifesto *The Experimental Novel* of 1880, Zola coined the term **naturalism** to describe a style that would document the real world as objectively and unsparingly as the century's own inventions, the phonograph and the camera – as did his own work, such as his novel *Germinal* (1885). The English novelist George Gissing (1857–1903) took up Zola's challenge with *The Nether World*, a harrowing story in which virtually all the characters are either corrupted by money or broken by poverty.

However, there was also a reaction against naturalism. The 1890s saw the rise of the station bookstalls run by companies such as

**CHECK THE BOOK**

Gissing's *The Nether World* tells the story of a man who tries to do good with a legacy but becomes a target for fortune hunters, while the enterprising Clara, who, like Sibyl Vane, tries to escape poverty via the stage, has acid thrown in her face by a rival and contracts a loveless marriage to survive. Its descriptions of the slums emulate Zola's.

W. H. Smith, and books published in a cheaper and more portable single-volume format to stock them. In this format modern **genre fiction** took shape: detective stories, notably those of Conan Doyle; adventure stories, such as those of Rider Haggard, whose exotic locations and tough (white) heroes were the prototype of the Indiana Jones movies; and what became known as science fiction, pioneered by H. G. Wells with stories of travel in time and space. It was also a period when folk and fairy tales were collected, documented and interpreted by scholars such as the anthropologist and historian Andrew Lang (1844–1912), whose *Blue Fairy Book* appeared in 1889, followed rapidly by the *Red*, *Yellow* and *Green Fairy Books*, all of which have remained in print.

A famous debate occurred in 1884 between Henry James, whose novels analysed the thought-processes of his educated and leisured characters in painstaking detail, and Robert Louis Stevenson, author of *Treasure Island*. James defended realism in his essay 'The Art of Realism' and Stevenson responded in favour of 'romance' in his essays 'A Gossip on Romance' and 'A Humble Remonstrance'. Wilde favoured Stevenson's side: in 'The Decay of Lying', published in the same year as *Dorian Gray*, he champions Zola's exposure of social evils but not his characters with 'their dreary vices and their drearier virtues ... who cares what happens to them?' (Holland, p. 974). Rather, he maintains that the artist should shape our understanding of the world and make us see it afresh: 'Life goes faster than Realism, but Romanticism is always in front of Life' (p. 992).

## THE VICTORIAN GOTHIC

The religious and scientific upheavals of the nineteenth century triggered a fascination with ghost stories and tales of terror, from those of Edgar Allan Poe (1809–49) in the United States to the work of the medievalist M. R. James in England (1862–1936). They all tapped into the Gothic tradition established in the previous century. Gothic novels, often set in the remote past, featured ghosts, mysteries and dreams in exotic castles and forests. Extreme emotions were expressed in extreme language, and there was a strong erotic element. While they allowed the reader to imagine a world free from everyday restraints, such novels were easily parodied. Jane Austen began writing her witty tale of a girl whose

> **CONTEXT**
>
> Until the rise of W. H. Smith's bookstalls, serious novels were first issued in a three-volume format. (Miss Prism in *The Importance of Being Earnest* is an amateur author, and in the last act it emerges that she mislaid the infant Jack in a handbag while filling his pram with 'the manuscript of a three-volume novel of more than usually revolting sentimentality'.) The cheaper single-volume edition appeared later, rather as a modern paperback follows a hardback. In 1895 Smith's and the biggest lending organisation, Mudie's Select Library, fixed prices and forced publishers to use the cheaper format for new fiction.

The Victorian Gothic continued

**CHECK THE BOOK**

In *She*, the 1887 novel by Henry Rider Haggard (1856–1925), an archaeologist travels with his ward Leo to a secret African world ruled by a mysterious white queen, Ayesha, who stays eternally young by bathing in a pillar of fire. Believing Leo to be the reincarnation of her lover, she urges him to bathe in the fire and become immortal too. When he hesitates, she steps into the fire a second time to encourage him, and at once withers and dies.

imagination runs away with her, *Northanger Abbey*, thirty-four years after the first of the genre, Walpole's *The Castle of Otranto*, was published in 1764.

The Victorians gave the Gothic a new lease of life by locating it in the modern world. In the most famous of all Victorian horror stories, Bram Stoker's *Dracula*, the vampire journeys from his Transylvanian castle to a world of typewriters, blood transfusions and railway engines. A similar Gothic modernity is found in a novel that profoundly influenced *Dorian Gray*: Stevenson's *The Strange Case of Dr Jekyll and Mr Hyde* (1886), the story of a doctor who develops a drug to isolate the 'good' aspects of his personality only to find that it releases a violent self, Mr Hyde. Jekyll is powerless to control Hyde, who grows stronger with every excess, while Jekyll weakens.

Like *Dorian Gray*, Stevenson's novel takes place in the modern city, from the slums to the houses of the wealthy hiding secrets behind closed doors. It explores degeneration: Jekyll feels a 'leap of welcome' (Stevenson, p. 79) as Hyde's personality takes over, suggesting that everybody carries the primitive within themselves. It also raises the possibility that the psyche might be not a unity but a collection of 'selves', what Jekyll calls 'a mere polity of multifarious, incongruous and independent denizens' (Stevenson, p. 76).

In 'The Decay of Lying' Wilde condemned the realistic treatment of Jekyll's research as 'dangerously ... like the *Lancet*' (Holland, p. 973), but this reflects his different approach to the relationship between character and environment. Jekyll moves in a circle of mild-mannered, socially responsible friends; Hyde is terrifying because he is unlike them. The possibility of a 'Hyde' within them remains just a possibility, although Stevenson's 'realism' hints that a means might be found to unleash it. Dorian, with his supernatural portrait, is frightening because he inhabits a world of predators and pleasure seekers like himself. As the only one who can evade the consequences of his actions, he enjoys watching others live out what might have been his own fate, from the opium-addicted Adrian Singleton to Lord Henry, 'wrinkled, and worn, and yellow' in his later years (p. 170).

Like earlier Gothic characters, Dorian encounters the horrors of bodily decay but, as Linda Dryden points out, Wilde's understanding of the function of this **imagery** is more sophisticated. While the pleasure of reading early Gothic novels lay in the way their external images of corruption played on our own unconscious fascination with death, here the forces that act on the painting 'as the worm … to the corpse' (Dryden, p. 132) are aspects of Dorian's own divided self; it is his subconscious, rather than ours, that is explored.

## DECADENTS AND SYMBOLISTS

Some time in the 1870s, the term 'decadents' was coined to describe a school of writers and artists who focused on the artificial and urban rather than the natural; by about 1885 they took to calling themselves Symbolists. The Decadents stretched the definition of beauty to encompass the grotesque, the dissident and the marginal. They considered that, rather than offering moral comment, the artist should embrace intensity of experience for its own sake. A key moment was the publication of Charles Baudelaire's (1821–67) book of poems *Flowers of Evil* in 1857, which scandalised the French literary establishment with its themes of death and sexuality.

Wilde met the man whom the French poets were later to call their 'prince', Paul Verlaine (1844–96), in Paris. Although slipping into alcoholism and drug addiction after the death of his lover, Verlaine had begun to push out the boundaries even further with his poetry about homosexual love. He also contended that poetry should avoid precise statement and gain its emotional power from the music of the verse and the carefully planned repetition of words and phrases for a hypnotic effect, an idea that clearly has its effect on passages in *Dorian Gray*.

## THE ENGLISH AESTHETICS

In England, the reaction against Victorian prudery and utilitarianism had begun with Matthew Arnold's 1857 Oxford lecture 'The Function of Criticism at the Present Time', calling for greater freedom of expression. This debate was taken up and developed at Oxford by Wilde's own tutors, Ruskin and Pater. Both stood against the insistence of the previous century that beauty equalled usefulness.

**CHECK THE FILM**

M. R. James's *Ghost Stories of an Antiquary* was published in 1904. For a number of years the BBC would broadcast a dramatisation of one of them at Christmas, the most famous being Jonathan Miller's production of *O Whistle and I'll Come to You, My Lad* in 1968, starring Michael Hordern as a scholar haunted by a shapeless horror after finding a whistle on a lonely beach.

Ruskin considered that 'the art of any country is the exponent of its social and political virtues' (from *The Library Edition of the Complete Works of John Ruskin*, ed. J. Dearden, 1903–12, Vol. 20, p. 39). He thought artists should have a prophetic function, helping humanity towards truths they could not grasp for themselves. While originally he perceived this to be within a Christian framework, the idea survived the loss of his faith and he continued to see art as a force for good, not because it was useful but because of its own intrinsic worth. In 1873 Pater's *The Renaissance* concluded with a burst of praise for sensuous rather than spiritual experience: 'To burn always with this hard, gemlike flame, to maintain this ecstasy, is success in life … the love of art for art's sake … to give nothing but the highest quality to your moments as they pass' (Mentor 1959 edition, p. 159).

While both were important to what became known as the Aesthetic Movement, neither Ruskin nor the timid Pater – 'Was he ever alive?' Wilde commented on hearing of his death (quoted in Ellmann, p. 50) – would have been entirely comfortable with its later work and its relationship to the French Symbolists. In 1866, for example, Algernon Charles Swinburne (1837–1909) explored masochism in the poem 'Dolores', with its refrain to 'Our Lady of Pain'. By 1894 the quarterly periodical *The Yellow Book* offered a range of poetry, short stories, essays, reproductions of paintings and specially commissioned artwork, by which the English Aesthetics could reach a wide audience for the cover price of five shillings. The young Aubrey Beardsley, its first art editor, who chose the yellow cover that linked it with French novels, became Wilde's chosen illustrator for *Salome*. His stark black and white images, simple, elegant and often obscene, were a marked contrast to the cluttered and sentimental work that filled the more conservative galleries, and provided a visual echo of the grotesque, anti-bourgeois and beautifully crafted poetry of the decadents. Wilde befriended several young decadent poets and paid for the publication of his lover John Gray's collection *Silverpoints*.

The most decisive Decadent influence on *Dorian Gray* was J. K. Huysmans's *A Rebours* (*Against Nature*). Published in 1884, it was identified at Wilde's trial as the book that corrupts Dorian Gray,

**CHECK THE BOOK**

You can read some of John Gray's poems, including one describing the 'leprous stain' of daisies on the grass, in *The Dedalus Book of English Decadence* (ed. J Willsher, 2004). The anthology also contains a useful preface tracing the origins of decadence from the eighteenth century onwards.

although this over-simplifies the complexity of the book and the relationship between it and Wilde's novel. A reaction against **naturalism**, it told the story of a man who embraces artifice and pleasure in all its forms. The last of an ancient and unhealthy dynasty, the hero, Des Esseintes, explores language, art, religion, sex and food. His pleasures are exotic. One of his many lovers is a ventriloquist who throws her voice into various images as she makes love. He fills his house with plants chosen because they look as if they have been man-made, and he builds an artificial seaside. He carries the Decadents' love of **synaesthesia**, the mixing of the senses, to new heights: one of his habits is to play a 'mouth-organ', a collection of carefully selected liqueurs whose tastes suggest a particular instrument of the orchestra. Increasingly, he becomes diseased. Syphilis and religious terror cause him pain, 'searing his innards with a red-hot iron' (Penguin translation by Robert Baldick, 1986 p. 93), and he cannot take ordinary food. The carefully researched, sensuous and darkly satirical presentation of exotic experience meant that the novel 'fell like a meteorite into the literary fairground, provoking anger and stupefaction', as the author put it (p. 10).

*Dorian Gray* contains definite echoes of *Against Nature*. Chapter 11 imitates Huysman's approach to a variety of arts: Dorian's study of perfumes in particular resembles that of Des Esseintes. However, there are significant differences. Des Esseintes exists in a kind of misanthropic vacuum. He makes his servants dress in monk-like robes, so that they become unnoticeable. He has few friends or conversations. His most extended human contact is with a boy he takes to a brothel, hoping that he will eventually take to crime to pay for his pleasure. Dorian has a more complex relationship with his world than the straightforward bitterness of Des Esseintes. He is less defiantly anti-bourgeois in his crimes – Des Esseintes sees the boy in the brothel as a kind of project to ruin society, while Dorian betrays and kills on impulse – but his relationship with his portrait prompts us to ask questions about the interaction between mind and body that the decay of Des Esseintes does not. The witty comments Wilde puts into the mouths of the social butterflies who form a chorus to Dorian's tragedy create a richer human context, and ensure that, despite drawing extensively on a variety of sources, the novel remains a true original.

**CONTEXT**

In *Against Nature*, Des Esseintes uses a variety of exotic stones to decorate the shell of a giant tortoise he has bought to contrast with his carpet. It promptly dies under the weight of cat's-eyes, rubies, turquoises and peridots.

**CHECK THE NET**

*The Official Website of Oscar Wilde* offers useful background material to Wilde's life and works, including photographs of the period. Go to **www. cmgworldwide.com/ historic/wilde/news. php**

## WILDE'S INFLUENCE

Wilde had tapped into a nineteenth-century obsession about the relationship between image and reality, and several works that followed were directly or indirectly influenced by *Dorian Gray*.

Violet Paget (1856–1935), who wrote under the name Vernon Lee, met Wilde on his honeymoon. *The Legend of Madame Krasinska*, published in 1892 and exploring the addiction to a personality mediated through a painted image, suggests she knew and admired *Dorian Gray*. A bored young widow owns a picture of a local character, Sora Lena, who has gone mad waiting for her sons, all dead in battle. The young woman attends a costume party dressed like the picture. Later she discovers that Sora Lena has committed suicide. Gradually she takes on the old woman's personality and appearance.

Edith Wharton (1862–1937), known for her subtle analysis of upper-class New Yorkers, also wrote some supernatural stories with echoes of *Dorian Gray*. *The Moving Finger,* published in 1901, is the story of a painter commissioned to paint a beautiful woman. After her death, her husband persuades him to retouch the picture so that his wife's image can age alongside him. When the husband dies, the artist restores the portrait to its youthful beauty, explaining, as Basil might explain his feelings for Dorian: 'You don't know how much of a woman belongs to you after you've painted her! There was one side of her … that was mine alone, and that was her beauty; for no one else understood it' (p. 36).

As one of the few easily available and popular texts to examine homosexual desire, *Dorian Gray* inevitably had an influence on subsequent novelists. E. M. Forster's *Maurice* was one of the first homosexual novels which allowed its central character to find happiness. Its structure, about a young man torn between two other men, owes something to *Dorian Gray*. Wilde himself makes a thinly veiled appearance in the novel as a slightly subversive figure who makes provocative remarks and is in general 'at play, but seriously' (Penguin 1971 edition, p. 34). Completed in 1914, *Maurice* had to wait until 1971 for publication.

## THE AFTER-LIFE OF DORIAN GRAY

The figure of Dorian Gray has fascinated people since Bosie first played up his personal resemblance to Wilde's hero. Its tragic structure and the dialogue Wilde found suitable for his own plays have made it a logical choice for dramatisation. However, cut loose from the extended passages of reflection, the story is ripe for re-interpretation and each version reflects its own times and **ideologies**.

The 1945 black-and-white film, written and directed by Albert Lewin, stressed the moral orthodoxy of the tale, with the tag-line: 'His life was a muddy morass into which he dragged all who knew him! Such was Dorian Gray, the man who wanted eternal youth, and bartered his soul to get it!' The satanic influence of Lord Henry was clear. George Sanders, a popular Hollywood **villain**, dominated the much younger Hurd Hatfield as Dorian. Rather than allowing Sibyl Vane an independent voice, the movie made her into a simple music-hall singer. Dorian, influenced by Lord Henry, asks her to stay the night: a test of virtue that she fails, and he rejects her. Contemplating the withered corpse of Dorian, Lord Henry mutters, 'God forgive me.' The heterosexuality of the characters is painstakingly established. Dorian is loved by Basil's niece, and there is a hint, as he utters a final prayer for mercy, that his soul is saved by the love of a good woman. If the morality of the film was orthodox, its treatment of the supernatural was not. The portrait of the young Dorian blossomed into Technicolor whenever it appeared, lighting up the screen. The changed portrait was not a realistic image of an individual but a partially abstract study of decay. Both images allowed Hurd Hatfield, a disciple of the Stanislavski school of realistic acting, to interact with his picture to convey genuine terror.

> **CONTEXT**
>
> The picture of the decaying Dorian was painted by Ivan Le Lorraine Albright and took approximately one year to complete. It is now owned by the Art Institute of Chicago. The portrait of the young Dorian was eventually given to Hurd Hatfield, who played him.

In contrast, John Osborne's adaptation for stage and television in 1973 stressed not satanic influence but the cult of youth. John Gielgud was an ageing Lord Henry, his hair dyed an unconvincing gold, hiding ever-deepening wrinkles with layers of makeup. Peter Firth as Dorian grew increasingly callous and brittle, and his exit, leaving Lord Henry alone and shivering in a fur coat, suggested that he did not so much resent him for 'poisoning his soul' as despise him as an old man. Dorian's transformation on death was less

**CHECK THE BOOK**

Dorian Gray makes a cameo appearance in Jasper Fforde's literary extravaganza *Lost in a Good Book* (2002), in which 'literary detective' Thursday Next polices the world of literature to ensure that characters do not wreck one another's texts. She encounters Dorian working as a used car salesman. His perfect vehicles contain a picture of an appalling old wreck in the boot.

terrifying (the corpse had put on a lot of weight) than this hardening of his personality.

Neil Bartlett's version at the Lyric, Hammersmith, in 1994 took yet another approach. It showed Wilde's friends, including the actress Ada Leverson, reading the novel together at the hotel where Wilde was arrested. Their interactions with a young guardsman and a maid, induced to play Dorian and Sibyl, brought out the class politics informing nineteenth-century attitudes to sexuality and power.

A radical interpretation by the company Show of Hands used two sets of actors in costume: one group vocalised the text, while the other performed in British Sign Language. This Dorian could never escape the presence of a double; the audience could never lose sight of the portrait. Constantly, we were implicitly asked to consider whether it was a mirror reflecting his 'real' self, or a *doppelganger* manipulating him into increasingly evil acts.

Will Self's 2002 novel *Dorian Gray: An Imitation* begins in 1981 – a year that the author suggests is 'peculiarly similar' to 1881 (the year Wilde published his poems), with its 'government at once regressive and progressive' (p. 3) – and ends with the death of Princess Diana in 1997, a century after Wilde left prison. Throughout the Thatcher years, Dorian, immortalised by 'Baz' Hallward in the video installation *Cathode Narcissus*, is a fabulous sexual and monetary success. Dorian contracts the AIDS virus at its height and his wilfully promiscuous behaviour has tragic results. Eventually his body is found in front of the video. But this ending proves to be the climax of a novel written by Lord Henry, now himself dead of AIDS. Lord Henry's ghost haunts the real Dorian, commenting acidly as Dorian smugly poses with New Labour celebrities. Dorian is finally killed by Ginger, the novel's equivalent of James Vane. While the action and the language of Self's novel might have shocked the Victorians, it takes a more generous view of humanity. Dorian is the only real **villain** of the story, loveless from beginning to end. Lord Henry shares a casual but lasting affection with his wife and Baz finds help and kindness from a trio of transvestites who wean him off drugs. Only Dorian swallows whole the capitalistic values of the eighties, expressed in both his real and his video bodies.

Matthew Bourne's ballet *Dorian Gray,* first performed at Sadler's Wells in 2008, located the magic of the portrait in the celebrity of its subject. Dorian is the 'face of a new fragrance', his image visible everywhere as an icon of sexual and commercial desire. Fame, not Basil the photographer or 'Lady H', his predatory patroness, corrupts Dorian. As his image inflames the desires of his public, Dorian grows violent. Corpses decorate his room; he is haunted, not by a changing portrait but by a mocking *doppelganger,* the outward sign of his disintegrating self. The power of this version lay in its tension between story and medium. Ballet shows the dancer working at a peak of bodily perfection to make a movement beautiful: the contrast between the dancer's body and the realistic violence of the acts it simulated (rare in ballet) told, as Matthew Bourne put it, 'an ugly story about beauty'.

If all these adaptations have radically changed both characters and action, they are still driven by the haunting figure of Dorian Gray. Leaving prison, Wilde received a gift, a story by the novelist and critic Max Beerbohm. *The Happy Hypocrite* is the tale of a man who wears a pleasant mask until he becomes pleasant himself. Wilde wrote to Beerbohm, 'The implied and accepted recognition of *Dorian Gray* in the story cheers me. I had always been disappointed that my story had suggest no other work of art in others' (Hart-Davis, p. 275). As his hero continues to appear in novels, films, opera, ballet and graphic novels, Wilde has no reason to feel disappointed.

> **CONTEXT**
>
> In Irish legend Oscar was a magical prince born to the fairy Niamh and the mortal warrior-poet Ossian, who goes to live with her in Tir Nan Og. Riding to visit the land of his ancestors after three centuries, Ossian accidentally touches his native earth and instantly loses his youthful immortality, his white beard sweeping the ground.

## World events

**1854** Founding of University College Dublin

**1855** David Livingstone discovers Victoria Falls

**1856** Louis Pasteur discovers bacteria

**1857** Opium war with China re-opened

**1858** Fenian (Irish Republican) Brotherhood founded

**1859** Bishop Colenso denies authenticity of the Pentateuch

**1860** Lord Elgin takes Beijing

**1861** American Civil War begins

**1862** Giuseppe Garibaldi attempts unification of Italy

**1863** Abraham Lincoln signs Emancipation Proclamation

**1864** Pius IX writes *Syllabus of Errors* attacking socialism, rationalism, divorce, etc.

**1865** Prison Act imposes rules of silence

**1866** Transatlantic telegraph cable laid

**1867** Second Reform Act

## Oscar Wilde's life

**1854** Wilde born in Dublin

**1867** Death of Wilde's sister Isola, aged eight

## Literary/artistic events

**1854** Coventry Patmore, *The Angel in the House*

**1855** Walt Whitman, *Leaves of Grass*

**1856** Death of Robert Schumann

**1857** Charles Baudelaire, *Les Fleurs du Mal*

**1858** Reuter's gets its first newspaper client, the London *Morning Advertiser*

**1859** Alfred Tennyson, *Idylls of the King*; death of Thomas De Quincey

**1860** George Eliot, *The Mill on the Floss*

**1861** Charles Dickens, *Great Expectations*

**1862** Victor Hugo, *Les Misérables*

**1863** Baudelaire's last poems

**1864** Matthew Arnold, 'The Function of Criticism at the Present Time'

**1865** John Ruskin, *Sesame and Lilies*

**1866** A. C. Swinburne, *Poems and Ballads*

**1867** Paris Exhibition

## World events

**1868** Last public execution in England

**1869** Girton College founded

**1870** First Married Women's Property Act

**1871** Paris Commune suppressed

**1872** Ballot Act makes voting secret

**1873** Custody of Infants Act

**1874** Benjamin Disraeli wins major election victory and leads Conservative reforming government for next six years

**1875** Disraeli organises purchase of Suez Canal shares

**1876** Cesare Lombroso writes first study of criminology

**1877** Thomas Edison invents phonograph

**1878** Salvation Army formed

**1879** Irish National Land League

**1880** C. S. Parnell demands Home Rule for Ireland

## Oscar Wilde's life

**1871** Wins scholarship to Trinity College, Dublin

**1874** Wins Gold Medal for Greek at Trinity, and goes to Oxford

**1875** Visits Italy

**1876** Death of father; Wilde takes a first in Classical Moderations

**1877** Visits Greece

**1878** Graduates with First in *Litterae Humaniores* and wins Newdigate Prize for Poetry

**1879** Settles in London

## Literary/artistic events

**1868** Wilkie Collins, *The Moonstone*

**1869** Leo Tolstoy, *War and Peace*

**1870** Death of Dickens

**1871** Charles Darwin, *The Descent of Man*

**1872** Jules Verne, *Around the World in 80 Days*

**1873** Walter Pater, *Studies in the History of the Renaissance*

**1874** First Impressionist Exhibition in Paris

**1875** Tolstoy, *Anna Karenina*

**1876** Mark Twain, *Tom Sawyer*

**1877** August Rodin exhibits statues considered scandalously realistic

**1878** J. M. Whistler sues Ruskin

**1879** Henrik Ibsen, *A Doll's House*

**1880** Émile Zola, *Nana*

| World events | Oscar Wilde's life | Literary/artistic events |
|---|---|---|
| **1881** Czar Alexander II assassinated | **1881** *Poems* published | **1881** Gilbert and Sullivan, *Patience*, staged |
| **1882** Second Married Women's Property Act | **1882** US tour; *Vera* | **1882** Richard Wagner, *Parsifal* |
| **1883** Death of Karl Marx | **1883** Visits Paris | **1883** Friedrich Nietzsche, *Also Sprach Zarathustra* |
| **1884** Third Reform Act | **1884** Marries Constance Lloyd | **1884** J. K. Huysmans, *A Rebours* |
| **1885** Labouchère Amendment to the Criminal Law Act criminalises consenting homosexual acts in private | **1885** Son Cyril born | **1885** W. T. Stead, *The Maiden Tribute of Modern Babylon* |
| **1886** Charles Dilke in divorce scandal | **1886** Son Vyvyan born; meets Robert Ross | **1886** Robert Louis Stevenson, *The Strange Case of Dr Jekyll and Mr Hyde* |
| **1887** 'Bloody Sunday' riots; speed of light measured | **1887** Becomes editor of *Woman's World* | **1887** P. I. Tchaikovsky, *Swan Lake* |
| **1888** Whitechapel Murders | **1888** *The Happy Prince and Other Stories* | **1888** August Strindberg, *Miss Julie*; Nikolai Rimsky-Korsakov, *Scheherazade* |
| **1889** Cleveland Street scandal | **1889** *The Portrait of Mr W. H.* | **1889** G. B. Shaw, *Fabian Essays* |
| **1890** Parnell divorce scandal | **1890** First version of *Dorian Gray* published in *Lippincott's Magazine* | **1890** William James, *Principles of Psychology* |
| **1891** First skyscrapers built | **1891** *A House of Pomegranates*; *Lord Arthur Savile's Crime: Intentions*; 'The Soul of Man Under Socialism'; *The Picture of Dorian Gray*; *Salome* composed in French | **1891** Arthur Conan Doyle, *The Adventures of Sherlock Holmes* |

| World events | Oscar Wilde's life | Literary/artistic events |
|---|---|---|
| **1892** Keir Hardie elected as first socialist MP; formation of Independent Labour Party | **1892** *Lady Windermere's Fan* staged; *Salome* refused licence; meets Lord Alfred Douglas | **1892** Sigmund Freud, *A Case of Successful Treatment by Hypnotism* |
| **1893** Women get the vote in New Zealand; US stock market crash | **1893** *A Woman of No Importance* staged; blackmail attempt fails | **1893** Antonin Dvorak, *New World Symphony* |
| **1894** William Gladstone resigns; Sarah Grand coins term 'The New Woman' | **1894** Poem *The Sphinx*; *Salome* published | **1894** Claude Debussy, *Prelude à L'Après-midi d'un Faune* |
| **1895** X-rays discovered | **1895** *An Ideal Husband* staged; *The Importance of Being Earnest* staged; sues Marquess of Queensberry for libel; Wilde tried and sentenced to two years' hard labour | **1895** First films made; M. S. Nordau, *Degeneration* |
| **1896** Olympic Games revived after 1,500 years | **1896** Writes *De Profundis* | **1896** Alfred Jarry, *Ubu Roi*; H. G. Wells, *The Island of Dr Moreau* |
| **1897** Reuter's report atrocities in the Congo | **1897** Released and moves to France | **1897** Bram Stoker, *Dracula* |
| **1898** Marie and Pierre Curie discover radium | **1898** *The Ballad of Reading Gaol* published under name C.3.3; Constance Wilde dies | **1898** Death of Aubrey Beardsley |
| **1899** Boer War begins | **1899** Travels in Europe | **1899** Edward Elgar, *Enigma Variations* |
| | **1900** Dies 30 November in Paris | **1900** Death of Ruskin; Freud, *The Interpretation of Dreams* |

## USEFUL EDITIONS OF THE TEXT

Norton Critical Edition, ed. Donald Lawler, 1988
>Both versions of the text and a selection of critical material including excerpts from Pater's *The Renaissance* and Huysman's *A Rebours*

Oxford University Press 1974 edition, ed. Isobel Murray
>Some useful annotations and a detailed examination of some of Wilde's sources

## ESSAYS, STORIES AND CRITICISM

*The Complete Works of Oscar Wilde*, ed. Merlin Holland, Collins, 1998
>Contains *De Profundis*, *The Portrait of Mr W. H.*, Wilde's short stories, *The Ballad of Reading Gaol* and 'The Soul of Man Under Socialism', as well as play texts including *Salome*

## LETTERS

*The Selected Letters of Oscar Wilde*, ed. Rupert Hart-Davis, Oxford University Press, 1979

## PLAYS

*A Woman of No Importance*, New Mermaid, 2006

*Lady Windermere's Fan*, New Mermaid, 2006

*An Ideal Husband*, New Mermaid, 2006

*The Importance of Being Earnest*, New Mermaid, 2006

## BIOGRAPHICAL WORKS

Richard Canning, *Oscar Wilde*, Hesperus Press Brief Lives, 2008
  Short and accessible new biography which incorporates newest research

Richard Ellmann, *Oscar Wilde*, Penguin, 1990
  The standard biography; a well-written and absorbing text

H. Montgomery Hyde, *The Trials of Oscar Wilde*, Notable British Trials, William Hodge and Co., 1960
  Somewhat dated presentation, but incorporates Wilde's own words

Sheridan Morley, *Oscar Wilde*, Weidenfeld and Nicolson, 1976
  Very good source of visual material

Thomas Wright, *Oscar's Books*, Chatto & Windus, 2008
  Explores the man through his library

## CRITICAL WORKS

Neil Bartlett, *Who Was That Man? A Present for Mr Oscar Wilde*, Serpent's Tail, 1988
  Highly original – a confrontation between Wilde and a modern gay reader. Useful insights in a dramatic format

Neil Bartlett, *The Uses of Monotony: Repetition in the Language of Oscar Wilde, Jean Genet, Edmund White and Juan Gotisolo*, Birkbeck College, 1994
  Discussion of some of Wilde's linguistic tricks, with useful application to the role of Lord Henry

Karl Beckson, *Oscar Wilde: The Critical Heritage*, Routledge and Kegan Paul, 1970
  Presents generations of critical responses to all of Wilde's work – valuable in placing him in context

Laurel Brake, *Subjugated Knowledges: Journalism, Gender and Literature 1837–1907*, Palgrave Macmillan, 1994
  Includes an account of Wilde's time with *Woman's World*

Steven Bruhm, *Reflecting Narcissus: A Queer Aesthetic*, University of Minnesota Press, 2001
Difficult but rewarding study of the novel from a queer perspective

Linda Dryden, *The Modern Gothic and Literary Doubles: Stevenson, Wilde and Wells*, Palgrave, 2003
A very clear and lively insight into a major theme of the book

Regina Gagnier, *Idylls of the Marketplace: Oscar Wilde and the Victorian Public*, Scolar Press, 1987
Original study of Wilde through his relationship with his public

Bruce Michelson, *Literary Wit*, University of Massachusetts Press, 2000
Excellent analysis of the preface and a lively comparison of Wilde and Twain

Christopher Nassaar, *Into the Demon Universe: A Literary Exploration of Oscar Wilde*, Yale University Press, 1974
One of the first books to take Wilde seriously, though now somewhat dated

Lyn Pykett, *Reading Fin de Siècle Fictions*, Longman, 1996
Helpful introduction to the literature of the period

Peter Raby, *Oscar Wilde*, Cambridge University Press, 1988
Especially useful on the political implications of Wilde's work

Peter Raby (ed.), *The Cambridge Companion to Oscar Wilde*, Cambridge University Press, 1997
Helpful essays on Wilde, including a study of his relations with Victorian actresses

Neil Sammells, *Wilde Style: The Plays and Prose of Oscar Wilde*, Pearson Education, 2000
Lively postmodern account of Wilde

Alan Sinfield, *The Wilde Century: Effeminacy, Oscar Wilde and the Queer Moment*, Cassell, 1994
Explores attitudes to Victorian sexuality and how the figure of Wilde was used to construct the image of the homosexual

John Sloan, *Authors in Context: Oscar Wilde*, Oxford University Press, 2003
  Clear and helpful study that places Wilde in literary, historical and social context

Andrew Smith, *Victorian Demons: Medicine, Masculinity and the Gothic at the Fin de Siècle*, Manchester University Press, 2004
  Explores Wilde's use and development of the Gothic convention

Richard J. Walker, *Labyrinths of Deceit: Culture, Modernity and Identity in the Nineteenth Century*, Liverpool University Press, 2007
  Explores the idea of the double in this and other Victorian novels

Keith Womack, '"Withered, Wrinkled and Loathsome of Visage": Reading the Ethics of the Soul and Late Victorian Gothic in *The Picture of Dorian Gray*', in Ruth Robbins and Julian Wolfreys (eds), *Victorian Gothic,* Palgrave, 2000

## FICTION AND DRAMA

Neil Bartlett, *In Extremis*, Oberon, 2000

E. M. Forster, *Maurice*, Penguin, 1971

Theophile Gautier, *Mademoiselle de Maupin*, trans. Helen Constantine, Penguin, 2005

J. K. Huysmans, *Against Nature*, trans. Robert Baldick, Penguin, 1986

Vernon Lee, *Supernatural Tales*, ed. I. C. Willis, Peter Owen, 2004

Charles Maturin, *Melmoth the Wanderer*, World's Classics, 1989

Alan Moore, Kevin O'Neill, Ben Dimagmaliw and Bill Oakley, *The League of Extraordinary Gentlemen*, America's Best Comics, 2000

John Osborne, *The Picture of Dorian Gray: A Moral Entertainment*, Faber and Faber, 1973

Will Self, *Dorian: An Imitation*, Penguin, 2003

Robert Louis Stevenson, *The Strange Case of Dr Jekyll and Mr Hyde*, Broadview Literary Texts, 1999

Tom Stoppard, *The Invention of Love*, Faber and Faber, 1997

H. G. Wells, *The Time Machine*, Phoenix Paperback, 2004

H. G. Wells, *The Island of Doctor Moreau*, The Works of H.G. Wells, Vol. 2, Atlantic Edition, 1924

Edith Wharton, *The Demanding Dead*, ed. Peter Haining, Peter Owen, 2007

## VARIOUS

Peter Ackroyd, *London: The Biography*, Vintage, 2001

Walter Benjamin, *Illuminations*, trans. Harry Zohn, Jonathan Cape, 1968

Terry Eagleton, *Heathcliff and the Great Hunger*, Verso, 1995

Graham Hough, *The Last Romantics*, Duckworth, 1949

David Lodge, *Consciousness and the Novel*, Secker and Warburg, 2002

Francis O'Gorman, *Ruskin*, Sutton Pocket Biographies, Stroud, 1999

Judith Walkowitz, *City of Dreadful Delight: Narratives of Sexual Danger in Late Victorian London*, Virago, 1992

## WEBSITES

www.victorianweb.org – useful website on all things Victorian

www.vam.ac.uk/collections/index.html – website of the Victoria and Albert Museum (particularly useful for researching Chapter 11)

www.humnet.ucla.edu/humnet/clarklib/wildphot – photos of Wilde

**abjection**  the process of discarding violently a person or thing which repels (e.g. a corpse, excrement, or an enemy); the **abject** often becomes a source of fascination, prompting torture or abuse, rather than simply being ignored

**allegory**  a story or situation with two different meanings, where the characters and events symbolise a deeper meaning with moral or spiritual significance; the correspondences are precise

**allusion**  a passing reference in a work of literature to something outside the text; may include other works of literature, myth, historical facts or biographical detail

**ambiguous**  with the capacity to have double, multiple or uncertain meanings

**aphorism**  a short pithy saying

**cliché**  a widely used expression which, through over-use, has lost impact and originality

**comedy**  a story with a happy ending; most commonly, but not exclusively, used of plays

**crisis**  moment in a play or novel when tension reaches its peak

**dialogic form**  written as conversation

**direct speech**  speech reported as it is said by the speaker

**dénouement**  the point in the play where the whole plot has finally unfolded (from the French for 'untying a knot')

**development and complication**  the central section of a **well-made play** that makes the situation more complex and creates **suspense** about the outcome

**epigram**  a clever remark expressed in a witty and quotable way

**epiphany**  a moment of life-changing revelation

**euphemism**  an inoffensive word or phrase substituted for one considered offensive or harmful

**exposition**  the opening of a play in which is put over all the information that the audience needs in order to understand the situation

**Faustian bargain**  literally or metaphorically selling one's soul to gain a particular end

*flâneur*  figure frequently found in late nineteenth-century literature, a man of leisure who wanders the city streets observing life

**free indirect speech**  third-person **narrative** detailing the thoughts of a character, using their own distinctive language rather than that of an omniscient **narrator**

**genre fiction**  novels or stories that are aimed at a particular section of the market; for example, detective stories, science fiction or adventure stories

**ideology**  shared beliefs of a culture that are taken for granted and thus never questioned

**imagery**  descriptive language which uses images to make actions, objects and characters more vivid in the reader's mind

**indirect speech**  speech not directly reported but summarised, e.g. 'He said that ...'

**irony**  incongruity between what might be expected and what actually happens; the ill-timed arrival of an event that had been hoped for

**malcontent**  a character whose perceived lack of social position or advantage leaves them with a grudge against society and a desire to work mischief; common in the plays of the seventeenth century

**melodrama**  popular theatrical genre of the nineteenth century, distinguished by moralistic plots – often rooted in class struggle – with sensational effects

**metafiction**  fiction that is aware of its own status as a literary construct, even commenting upon it

**metaphor** a figure of speech in which a word or phrase is applied to an object, a character or an action which does not literally belong to it, in order to imply a resemblance and create an unusual or striking image in the reader's mind

**motivation** the desires and intentions that drive a character in naturalistic fiction to behave as they do

**narrative** a story, tale or any recital of events, and the manner in which it is told. First person narratives ('I') are told from the character's perspective and usually require the reader to judge carefully what is being said; second person narratives ('you') suggest the reader is part of the story; in third person narratives ('he, 'she', 'they') the **narrator** may be intrusive (continually commenting on the story), impersonal or omniscient. More than one style of narrative may be used in a text

**narrator** the voice telling the story or relating a sequence of events

**naturalistic, naturalism** style that tries to reflect the everyday world and its language

**omniscient narrator** a **narrator** who uses the third-person **narrative** and has a god-like knowledge of the thoughts and feelings of the characters

**orientalism** Western attitude to the East shaped by European imperialism

**pluperfect** the tense that expresses action completed in the past, using the word 'had'

**protagonist** the central character whose actions form the focus of the work

**realism** the literary portrayal of the 'real' world, in both physical and psychological detail, rather than an imaginary or ideal one; Victorian novels sometimes described themselves in this way

**resolution** final moments of a play in which the loose ends are tied up

**Romantic Movement** rebellion against the scientific rationalism and aristocratically based social order of the earlier eighteenth century in favour of politically radical art forms grounded in spontaneous feeling

**satire** literature in which folly, evil or contemporary issues are held up to scorn through ridicule, irony or exaggeration

**social comedy** comedy with an upper-class setting, noted for witty dialogue rather than physical jokes

**soliloquy** speech by a character alone on the stage, revealing their inner thoughts, feelings and intentions

**subtext** theatrical term to describe a pattern of emotions and energies that are not directly spoken about but show themselves through trivial actions or remarks that seem casual on the surface; it is a feature of naturalistic drama, and Wilde was a pioneer of the technique in England

**suspense** excitement about the outcome of the story, often raised to a high pitch just before a break in the action

**synaesthesia** the experience of mixing sensory perceptions – so 'hearing' colours as sounds, for example

**tableau, tableaux** if the situation at the end of an act was particularly striking, Victorian actors would briefly 'freeze' to allow the audience to take in the stage picture

**third person** see **narrative**

**villain** character responsible for the troubles of the **protagonist**

**well-made play** the form taken by most Victorian West End drama. A well made play has a clear structure: the **exposition** tells us what we need to know (usually that some of the characters have a secret ); the **development** brings the situation to **crisis** point, usually around the end of the penultimate act, as secrets come out and throw people into confusion; and finally there is a **resolution** in which all the loose ends are tied up

Frances Gray, formerly Reader in Drama at the University of Sheffield, has written widely on literature: her published books include titles on women, crime and language and Noël Coward. She is also a playwright, and has a Radio Times award for comedy. She is the author of the York Notes Advanced titles *A Woman of No Importance* and *A Doll's House*.

# NOTES

## GCSE

Maya Angelou
*I Know Why the Caged Bird Sings*

Jane Austen
*Pride and Prejudice*

Alan Ayckbourn
*Absent Friends*

Elizabeth Barrett Browning
*Selected Poems*

Robert Bolt
*A Man for All Seasons*

Harold Brighouse
*Hobson's Choice*

Charlotte Brontë
*Jane Eyre*

Emily Brontë
*Wuthering Heights*

Brian Clark
*Whose Life is it Anyway?*

Robert Cormier
*Heroes*

Shelagh Delaney
*A Taste of Honey*

Charles Dickens
*David Copperfield*
*Great Expectations*
*Hard Times*
*Oliver Twist*
*Selected Stories*

Roddy Doyle
*Paddy Clarke Ha Ha Ha*

George Eliot
*The Mill on the Floss*
*Silas Marner*

Anne Frank
*The Diary of a Young Girl*

William Golding
*Lord of the Flies*

Oliver Goldsmith
*She Stoops to Conquer*

Willis Hall
*The Long and the Short and the Tall*

Thomas Hardy
*Far from the Madding Crowd*
*The Mayor of Casterbridge*
*Tess of the d'Urbervilles*
*The Withered Arm and other Wessex Tales*

L. P. Hartley
*The Go-Between*

Seamus Heaney
*Selected Poems*

Susan Hill
*I'm the King of the Castle*

Barry Hines
*A Kestrel for a Knave*

Louise Lawrence
*Children of the Dust*

Harper Lee
*To Kill a Mockingbird*

Laurie Lee
*Cider with Rosie*

Arthur Miller
*The Crucible*
*A View from the Bridge*

Robert O'Brien
*Z for Zachariah*

Frank O'Connor
*My Oedipus Complex and Other Stories*

George Orwell
*Animal Farm*

J. B. Priestley
*An Inspector Calls*
*When We Are Married*

Willy Russell
*Educating Rita*
*Our Day Out*

J. D. Salinger
*The Catcher in the Rye*

William Shakespeare
*Henry IV Part I*
*Henry V*
*Julius Caesar*
*Macbeth*
*The Merchant of Venice*
*A Midsummer Night's Dream*
*Much Ado About Nothing*
*Romeo and Juliet*
*The Tempest*
*Twelfth Night*

George Bernard Shaw
*Pygmalion*

Mary Shelley
*Frankenstein*

R. C. Sherriff
*Journey's End*

Rukshana Smith
*Salt on the Snow*

John Steinbeck
*Of Mice and Men*

Robert Louis Stevenson
*Dr Jekyll and Mr Hyde*

Jonathan Swift
*Gulliver's Travels*

Robert Swindells
*Daz 4 Zoe*

Mildred D. Taylor
*Roll of Thunder, Hear My Cry*

Mark Twain
*Huckleberry Finn*

James Watson
*Talking in Whispers*

Edith Wharton
*Ethan Frome*

William Wordsworth
*Selected Poems*

*A Choice of Poets*

*Mystery Stories of the Nineteenth Century including The Signalman*

*Nineteenth Century Short Stories*

*Poetry of the First World War*

*Six Women Poets*

For the AQA Anthology:
*Duffy and Armitage & Pre-1914 Poetry*

*Heaney and Clarke & Pre-1914 Poetry*

*Poems from Different Cultures*

## Key Stage 3

William Shakespeare
*Much Ado About Nothing*
*Richard III*
*The Tempest*

Margaret Atwood
*Cat's Eye*
*The Handmaid's Tale*

Jane Austen
*Emma*
*Mansfield Park*
*Persuasion*
*Pride and Prejudice*
*Sense and Sensibility*

Pat Barker
*Regeneration*

William Blake
*Songs of Innocence and of Experience*

The Brontës
*Selected Poems*

Charlotte Brontë
*Jane Eyre*
*Villette*

Emily Brontë
*Wuthering Heights*

Angela Carter
*The Bloody Chamber*
*Nights at the Circus*
*Wise Children*

Geoffrey Chaucer
*The Franklin's Prologue and Tale*
*The Merchant's Prologue and Tale*
*The Miller's Prologue and Tale*
*The Pardoner's Tale*
*The Prologue to the Canterbury Tales*
*The Wife of Bath's Prologue and Tale*

Caryl Churchill
*Top Girls*

John Clare
*Selected Poems*

Joseph Conrad
*Heart of Darkness*

Charles Dickens
*Bleak House*
*Great Expectations*
*Hard Times*

John Donne
*Selected Poems*

Carol Ann Duffy
*Selected Poems*
*The World's Wife*

George Eliot
*Middlemarch*
*The Mill on the Floss*

T. S. Eliot
*Selected Poems*
*The Waste Land*

Sebastian Faulks
*Birdsong*

F. Scott Fitzgerald
*The Great Gatsby*

John Ford
*'Tis Pity She's a Whore*

John Fowles
*The French Lieutenant's Woman*

Michael Frayn
*Spies*

Charles Frazier
*Cold Mountain*

Brian Friel
*Making History*
*Translations*

William Golding
*The Spire*

Thomas Hardy
*Jude the Obscure*
*The Mayor of Casterbridge*
*The Return of the Native*
*Selected Poems*
*Tess of the d'Urbervilles*

Nathaniel Hawthorne
*The Scarlet Letter*

Homer
*The Iliad*
*The Odyssey*

Khaled Hosseini
*The Kite Runner*

Aldous Huxley
*Brave New World*

Henrik Ibsen
*A Doll's House*

James Joyce
*Dubliners*

John Keats
*Selected Poems*

Philip Larkin
*High Windows*
*The Whitsun Weddings and Selected Poems*

Ian McEwan
*Atonement*

Christopher Marlowe
*Doctor Faustus*
*Edward II*

Arthur Miller
*All My Sons*
*Death of a Salesman*

John Milton
*Paradise Lost Books I and II*

George Orwell
*Nineteen Eighty-Four*

Sylvia Plath
*Selected Poems*

William Shakespeare
*Antony and Cleopatra*
*As You Like It*
*Hamlet*
*Henry IV Part I*
*King Lear*
*Macbeth*
*Measure for Measure*
*The Merchant of Venice*
*A Midsummer Night's Dream*
*Much Ado About Nothing*
*Othello*
*Richard II*
*Richard III*
*Romeo and Juliet*
*The Taming of the Shrew*
*The Tempest*
*Twelfth Night*
*The Winter's Tale*

Mary Shelley
*Frankenstein*

Richard Brinsley Sheridan
*The School for Scandal*

Bram Stoker
*Dracula*

Alfred Tennyson
*Selected Poems*

Virgil
*The Aeneid*

Alice Walker
*The Color Purple*

John Webster
*The Duchess of Malfi*
*The White Devil*

Oscar Wilde
*The Importance of Being Earnest*
*The Picture of Dorian Gray*
*A Woman of No Importance*

Tennessee Williams
*Cat on a Hot Tin Roof*
*The Glass Menagerie*
*A Streetcar Named Desire*

Jeanette Winterson
*Oranges Are Not the Only Fruit*

Virginia Woolf
*To the Lighthouse*

William Wordsworth
*The Prelude and Selected Poems*

Wordsworth and Coleridge
*Lyrical Ballads*

*Poetry of the First World War*